"Suzanne is our secon̲⎯⎯⎯⎯⎯⎯⎯ creative in writing and drawing since an early age. This book is a wonderful success story of her life and expressing her faith in God. We are very proud of her and her accomplishments. She has grown into a fine woman and mother. May God bless you who read this." —*Mom*

"*Following God's Footprints* is a wonderful life story filled with touching memories. From tragedy to new life and new beginnings, through the birth of a first child and loss of a wonderful husband and father, you are led on a journey which reminds the heart that all moments in life are seeds being planted for future growth." —*Audry Pasqua, niece*

"Suzy's book is honest, insightful, and will make you laugh! Her story could be described as a beautiful blossoming of personal strength and maturity. Through tragedies she finds that God is with her at every step of the way. You will find her writing relatable and joyful." —*Lisa Favor*

"What is your legacy as a Christian? Who have you influenced by your walk with Christ? How have you taught your children to find joy, peace, strength, and love through their walk with God? What can we learn from Suzy's personal journey that applies to our life? Read her story of love and acceptance; you too may find yourself doing a bit of introspection and re-prioritizing."
—*Chris Gowins*

# Contents

I want to humbly thank God for having the
ability to write my thoughts down.

My father and mother who taught me to have faith,
sharing their love unconditionally.

My precious husband, Norm, who took me out of
being lost and brought me back to being found
with Jesus Christ as my Savior.

My grown adults, Nichole, Bryan, Brittany and Sarah
as they are a blessing in my life, parenting them
is a large piece of who they are today.

Lastly, to my close family of believers, who have showered me
with love, wisdom, and discernment
during life's unexpected challenges.

# Introduction

In 2019, when I began writing my book, *Following God's Footprints*, I had no intention of going as far as publishing my thoughts. At the top of my first page, I wrote the question, "Why...God?" I'm sure we can think of many situations that cause us to question why something has happened each and every day. At that time in my life, I wanted to keep my mind occupied, trying not to think too much about the trials I was experiencing.

I wrote in detail about situations that unraveled throughout my growing years. I took my journal or book almost every place I went to record in detail the experiences in my past, which flew through my mind often quicker than my fingers could write. Countless Bible verses came to mind and helped me, significantly relating to the direction on which I was focused.

A few months after beginning to scribble my memories down, I walked on the next "bridge" in my life, allowing the Holy Spirit to continually engage me while writing. I decided to put my memories into a book for my kids to read in the future. I never dreamt that *Following God's Footprints* would be published, and I would be speaking to a group of people, sharing my growth, and reaching out to my readers.

Memories I have written about record my journey as a young, determined girl, growing up with three siblings. I tried to be independent with responsibilities, yet too often looked for approval and depended on others to be in charge. As I grew older, I began feeling the desire to know the Lord. He used messages, songs, and the Bible to plant seeds of faith during my life's journey. God faithfully continued to water and give these seeds of faith light, but I felt this only when I closed "my umbrella" and allowed my life to be nourished by God's love.

In this book, I share an experience when life took an unexpected turn, and I had to begin a lifestyle for which I was unprepared. I felt like I was beginning again from scratch. God came aboard and re-sprouted His seeds of life and growth, though differently from what hospital specialists had diagnosed. I was involved in a car accident in 1984, finishing my second year at UCSD. Recovery began with intense weeks, leading to long, depressing months. I still had no hope for my future, yet God had other plans for me.

In writing, I included fun experiences, struggles, challenging events, depression, angry tears, and also blessings, for which I am thankful. God never left me and was by my side, even if I wasn't always aware of His presence. I met my husband, Norm, and we continued attending a Catholic church where I was raised and where we were happily married. I began slowly not to be as eager to attend church each week, and Norm continued to go by himself. After being married for a few years, together we began seeking for a church in which to raise our future family.

*Start children off in the way they should go, and even when they are old, they will not turn from it* (Proverbs 22:6).

I relived other devastating trials repeatedly as time progressed. I faced difficult circumstances as doctors saw that my husband had serious health conditions involving many future rough roads within our family. I proceeded with my stronghold of faith and determination, resting assured, though at various times, ignoring God's existence or showing a lack of humility and trust in His plans.

Through suffering with the ones close to my heart, reality stepped in, after hopeless grief, with slow thoughts for my future ahead, and later stretching out for self-pity and idols taking the place of God. I began turning my life and hopes in a direction I later found out were not in His timing, His presence, or following my spiritual path.

Reading the book of Genesis in the Bible, I see how God was disappointed with how His creation became corrupt. He instructed Noah to build an ark and take with him onboard his family, along with one male and one female of all animals and creatures. When Noah had finished doing as God told him to do, the flood arose, and the earth vanished for 150 days, yet Noah and all aboard the ark were safe! Genesis 7:5 reads: "And Noah did ALL that the Lord commanded him."

Now in my 50s, closer to reaching 60, I feel I have accomplished goals that I didn't think possible before God's "ark" rebuilt my life and kept me safe. Today I see our world continually facing battles the same as it did in the beginning of creation. There are personal trials, health issues, anxiety, depression, fires, floods, hurricanes, earthquakes, and many more material obstacles we are challenged with each day.

I desire to be a person like Noah, whom the Spirit gathers, reinforces, and guides to help grow closer to Him. This was the meaning behind my confidence in finishing my life's story. I want my past, my challenges, my happy times, and my oh so hopeless times to help those in need of a reason to go on with their presence.

I hope *Following God's Footprints* will challenge those who want to take a humongous step as Noah did in building the ark and as I have in writing my book. Miss Shy Suzy never thought I would be in this position to encourage others and to let people know they too can be like Noah, building an ark as a refuge from the "storms," to bring themselves and those around them deeper into God's blessings.

I see I have grown so much in my spiritual life, and I feel led to share my life experiences. God teaches us throughout the Bible that we need to share our faith and expand in our beliefs with the ultimate goal of bringing people to know Him. Realizing how the Spirit is continually working through me to share my faith through my manuscript brings me so much happiness.

God wants you and me to grow in our lives daily. We will have eternal life with Him one day. Growth happens by allowing the Holy Spirit, with His many seeds, to bring forth the light in our unsure world today. God plants seeds in our lives, and I pray that your path may be uncovered. I want to share how God brought me through life situations that were out of my control. I would not have become the thriving Christian woman I am today if I had not accepted Jesus as my Lord and Savior.

Similar to how God reached me through seeds that didn't seem to be sprouting at certain times when I wanted them to, I have faith that God will use this book for His glory. It is my turn now to reach out to others experiencing difficulties and trials, who are digging for hope, growing apart from God, or wanting to find that "light" and "water" needed to plant and nourish their seeds.

I pray *Following God's Footprints* will touch others as my writing has captured my faith in ways that I never imagined were possible. I see my book honoring the words Joy, Hope and Peace, and I pray that these words may bring the Holy Spirit deeper into your life. God has plans for each of us, as shown through numerous Bible verses, answering my question at the beginning of my book and also in this message today of *Why…God?*

I want to read a quote I found in a book called *Grace for the Moment* by Max Lucado. The message is titled, "The Ultimate Triumph."

> What we see as the ultimate tragedy, he sees as the ultimate triumph. And when a Christian person dies, it's not a time to despair but a time to trust. The seed buried in the earth will blossom in heaven. Your soul and body will reunite, and you will be like Jesus.

*Grace for the Moment* was given to me soon after my husband passed away, and I began to read it as my daily devotion. It certainly helped me reach out daily for my living Savior and lead me down my future path as a single Christian woman.

I began writing my book two and a half years after Norm went to heaven. I mentioned in the last chapter simple, yet meaningful advice given to me by an elderly woman I met at church, who also was a widow. She stared into my crying eyes and told me peacefully to "Let God be my date!" This made a strong impact on me to try and walk deeper in His footprints.

Lastly, here is a quote from the book *Jesus in Me* by Anne Graham Lotz:

> Your entire life's experience is worthwhile and can be used to make an eternal impact in the life of someone else. The Holy Spirit can so flood us with God's grace that we are quickened to look beyond ourselves -our own pain and suffering or our own happiness and success- to reach out and help someone else.

I pray that by reading *Following God's Footprints,* you too can look to God to guide your path beyond life's trials so that you may also reach out and touch someone with your faith!

# ⮑1⮐

# Fearfully and Wonderfully Made

I wondered, *God, why do You put trials and tribulations in my life, and how do these moments bring me closer to You?* Well, I thought I would write about the last nearly fifty-six years of my life and the journey that explains my relationship with God, which has certainly answered that question I often ask myself.

I was born on April 7, 1964, at St Francis Hospital in Lynwood, California. I had a sister, Sherrie, who was two years and four months older than me. Our family of four—my mother and father, my sister and me—moved to Placentia, California, when I was six months old, where my parents purchased their first home.

When I was almost two and a half years old, another sister came into our family. Her name was Laura, and she was born on August 16, which was our dad's birthday as well. As she was getting close to six months old, my parents noticed she was not developing at a normal pace. They had her checked by a doctor, and by the time she was a year old, it was determined that she was mentally and physically handicapped. My parents were advised to put her in an institution and pretend they had never had her.

Of course, Laura stayed as an active part of our family, but she needed a lot of attention, therapy, time, patience, love, nurture, and care. My parents were willing to give all of this to her! They look to her as their angel to this day, and I believe God blessed our family with her to bring us closer to each other. The

1

example my parents gave to me, and the gift that Laura is, inspired me to pursue the career that I still enjoy today.

My first day of school, in kindergarten, was at Wagner Elementary School, in Placentia. My mother made sure I was wearing a pretty dress and that my very blond hair was put up in two curly pigtails. This I know just from seeing a photo of myself with a neighborhood boy whom I posed next to for a picture—in which I had a noticeably huge smile. I might have been excited because I was starting school, or he could have been my first "heartbeat for a boy."

Most of my growing-up years were spent at the house in Placentia. Sherrie and I were allowed to take groceries from the cabinet and set up a pretend "grocery store." We played house with one another for hours, one of us shopping and the other at the pretend cash register. We played dress-up a lot, which I vaguely remember but was told about by my mom recently.

I also remember playing with baby dolls and Barbie dolls a lot. One day I decided to trim Sherrie's favorite doll's hair. After I did so, she discovered her doll and then proceeded to cut my hair because she was so angry! We often got upset with one another, and I can distinctly see us upstairs in the hall, with her arms reaching out to scratch me as I forcefully hit her. These types of things can happen between two sisters throughout childhood.

When I was almost six years old, my uncle came to move in with us at the age of ten. He was my mom's stepbrother, and a short time before, he had been away in Big Bear with his parents and my mom's other brother. Both of my uncles were out fishing at Big Bear Lake when my grandma—my mother's mom—and my step-grandpa died in a sudden fire while in their cabin. I'm sure it was a hard time for my mom to mourn the sudden death of her mother while also accepting the responsibility of a new child. In 1971, we moved into a larger home in Placentia to accommodate our growing family.

I began my second grade at a new school, Golden Elementary. I tried my hardest to get good grades all throughout my growing-up years. I am not sure if I wanted to be a "good example" to my parents and teachers, or if I was just trying not to cause any further problems, stress, or worries at home. I remember that when I was around this age—seven or eight—my father would teach a catechism class to a large group of friends in my grade from St. Joseph's church at our home. This might have been when some seeds were planted that would affect my future walk with God.

As I grew up, Mom enrolled Sherrie and me in the Indian Maidens, an organization like the Girl Scouts, and we participated in many of their activities. We were in the Zuni tribe and would go to meetings once a month, where we would complete an artwork project and go on outings. We also marched together in parades with other tribes of the Indian Maidens.

Mom played a very meaningful part in my life as I grew up. She often could be found cleaning the house, ironing, sewing costumes, mending buttons, hemming pants, or cooking. When she was busy cleaning, I would have to watch out because she was often never in a particularly good mood. She also would frequently wear a colorful scarf covering her hairdo when she cleaned, so when she had a scarf on, "Watch out!" When she was not busy with those chores or cooking—usually at the same time!—she would test us kids on our spelling words or ask questions for the tests we had coming up in school. Mom spent quality time reading and playing games with us in front of the TV.

When I was almost ten years old, a surprise pregnancy added to our already busy family of five. Later that year, my brother, Donald, was born. I remember my dad's big smile as he woke up Sherrie and me. We were sleeping in our corner group bed when he woke us and told us that Mom had delivered a son into the Palmer family!

In the sixth grade, I had a difficult teacher, and I cried when I did not get an A on all the work I had turned in or on tests I had taken. I certainly was happy to move on to Tuffree Middle School. One of my teachers would wait each day until the class was quiet. She then would proceed to say in front of the class, "Hello, Miss Suzy," and I would respond back to her "hello," following with her name. We both would smile, and then the class would proceed.

In both seventh and eighth grade, I tried out for the cheerleading squad, but I did not make it either year. As a result, my mother complained to the principal that I had much better grades than those who did make the squad. Nothing resulted from my mom's visit to the school, and I spent about two days pouting about the situation.

Each year of junior high, I also tried out for the drill team, and it was quite easy to make the squad there. I practiced during the week and went marching in parades, as my parents watched me show off my talents. I watched my mom as she made my uniform to march in. My parents were supportive and involved with me all throughout my school years, going to parades as well as the spelling bees I often participated in.

In the seventh grade, I was accepted into a "Leadership" class, taught and led by a special teacher. We had the privilege of putting together the yearbook each year (I was also in this class in eighth grade). In this seventh-grade class, I met a popular girl named Lisa. I envied her continuous smile and wished I could be as popular as she was.

I went on my first "date" with a boy in seventh grade. Of course, his parents drove us on our date to get ice cream. When we were driven back to my house, he walked me up to the door and said good night.

I was a good student who spent most of my time doing my homework and additional assignments for extra credit. This probably was the reason I was able to take Algebra in the eighth grade, since there were very few who were accepted into this class before high school. I did quite well in the class, and I still have a clear image of my teacher's smiling face.

I had an art class in seventh grade and possibly also in eighth grade that I really enjoyed and where I learned a lot of artistic skills. I got to know my friend Lisa a lot better then, as well, since she was in the class too.

On the last day of junior high, I took a photo with a boy I thought was awfully cute. I was able to not wear my glasses for the picture because I now had contact lenses! Next up was struggling through four long years of braces!

When I was thirteen years old, I began to babysit. I was finally becoming more independent and making decisions as a young teenager.

One year our entire family took a vacation in a motor home, traveling for a month across the United States. We went as far east as Dixon, Illinois, and then we returned home through Houston, Texas. At each of these two locations, we visited with relatives on both sides of the family. Along the way, we stopped off in Wisconsin Dells to eat at Paul Bunyan's restaurant! We ate chicken at a large bench-style table and afterward had a LONG evening ahead. All six of us endured food poisoning in this small, enclosed motor home. What a memory!

# 2

## Straying Footprints

I had become a young teenager, turning over a chapter in my life and beginning the next phase... El Dorado High School, here I come! Before I began my freshman year, I tried out again for cheerleading, and this time I made it to the "runners-up" stage in the process. Ultimately, however, I did not make the squad. Almost, but not quite!

In high school, I found out that my friend Lisa, whom I had met in Leadership and in art class, lived right down the street from me with her aunt, uncle, and two cousins. We got to know each other much better in high school. We were in Spanish 1 class together, and the class was a joke! We both sat in the back row, chatting away, as we had a teacher who taught us absolutely nothing.

One cute guy would always sneak in late and sit in the back row right next to Lisa and me. The teacher would get angry with him for being tardy, but he would never do anything about it. This cute guy would ask Lisa and me, usually toward the end of the week, where all the parties were happening over the weekend. We would happily let him know, hoping to see him there.

Surprisingly, later that year, we found out that this "cute guy" was actually an undercover cop—and he was the one getting in trouble in class and being kicked out quite often! We finally caught on to the scheme when this cute guy was no longer in the class and the parties were not continually getting broken up as they had been before.

During freshman year, I hung out a lot with Lisa. On the

weekends we would go to parties, and we even hit some fraternity parties at Cal State Fullerton. We would usually go party-hopping with my sister Sherrie and her friend, after drinking a few too many beers.

Although we were not supposed to leave our high school campus during school hours, we often did during assemblies. This happened a lot during my years in high school. We would choose one of our homes to hang out at—which usually ended up being Lisa's house. We would pig out on breakfast pancakes, waffles, cookies, and candy—you name it, we ate it. After so much eating, we would go running after school at Tri-City Park to burn off the calories.

Lisa and I had a lot of good times together, but we could also end up getting in arguments after school…and depending on whose house we were at, one or the other of us would angrily stomp back home. Soon after that, we would call each other, cry over the phone, and say how sorry we were. We were "hanging out" buddies during most of our freshman year.

Also, during my freshman year in 1978, I experienced my first crush on a guy—and my first kiss. Of course, not being sixteen years old yet, I could not go on a date with him. He was a senior at El Dorado High, and he was friends with a guy whom I had met at St. Joseph's, the church my family attended. My sister Sherrie and I were friends with both of them, and the four of us would often hang out.

One night I was out driving with Sherrie and these two guys in my parents' Jaguar. We had already been drinking a lot. Around midnight, we were heading down Palm Drive in Placentia, with the golf course on our right. Suddenly a very tall tree crashed down on the road, right in front of our car, landing on the ground and covering more than half of the street. Sherrie came to an immediate stop, and we all freaked out due to the sudden interference of the tree.

Sherrie turned left into a park nearby. We got out and headed toward the restrooms, but as we entered, we were then shocked by yet something else. Wet blood covered each of the restroom stalls, and we all freaked out even more. At that point we decided to call it a night. The sporadic relationship with that senior guy I'd had a crush on did not last a long time.

Before my sophomore year began, I became friends with another girl my age from high school. We both loved hanging out at Newport Beach during the summer, and we had something else in common. We both enjoyed being "different" from those around us. We had a habit of growing our hair out on our legs and then spraying bleach on our legs before lying out on the sand. What beach bums we were! HAHA!

One day as we were at Newport sunning our hairy legs, we were checking out a couple of cute guys there. When we began talking with them, we learned that one boy's father had founded the famous department store at that time called "May Company." Wow, in our eyes we had just met a celebrity! We asked him and his cute friend if they would mind teaching us how to surf with their surfboards. They agreed, and we flirty girls each took a board, tucked it under our arms, went out into the water until it reached our knees, and then immediately headed back to the shore! That was about as risky as we both wanted to be!

I don't remember much from my sophomore year. I do know that I tried out for the dance team for El Dorado High and made it! I was so excited! I looked forward to practicing and participating in several performances for the school. Lisa was also on the dance team. We spent a lot of time during classes and rehearsals practicing for the large productions. The teacher was quite strict and she made us work hard, but I did enjoy it, and our class had a lot of laughs together.

When I turned sixteen years old, it was finally time for me to go out into the "real world" and find a job! I began working at

Norton's Palm Cleaners. I worked behind the counter when customers would come in, or I helped toward the back hanging up, tagging, and putting clothing in plastic bags. It was a somewhat boring, often slow job, but one specific incident stuck in my mind. I was behind the counter waiting to help the next customer, and guess who walked in to pick up his police uniform? Yes, it was the cute undercover cop who had sat next to Lisa and me in class during our freshman year! Yes, it was the same policeman who always managed to shut down the best parties in town. Hahaha!

As I mentioned before, my family was Catholic, and each week we went to church together at St. Joseph's. I also went to a weekly high school Bible study. Every summer, we would also go as a group to Campus by the Sea in Catalina. It was a fun summer day camp that lasted a week, where I learned more about God and my friends—and I also tried to pick up the cute guys working there. Our weekly excursion to Avalon was a dreadfully long hike. We took off early in the morning on a four-hour journey to freedom for the day! We would hang out with old and new friends we had met at camp and check out all the locals hanging around in town at Avalon.

Back at church, there was one certain guy I thought was awfully cute. His name was, we will say, Fred. Yes, I obviously was not getting much out of each week's sermon; I was going to church for just one reason. I wanted to bump into that guy I had a crush on! I found out he worked at Ralph's grocery store nearby, so whenever Mom needed any groceries, I was glad to go run the errand for her!

On one such errand, I saw Fred bagging groceries, so I chose the register line where he was working. I was only purchasing a few items, like bananas, ketchup, and mustard, and of course, Fred cracked a joke: "So, are you going to be putting this ketchup and mustard on your bananas?" I began giggling at his sense of humor. I do remember we began dating shortly after that, in October of my junior year. He was my very first boyfriend, and he meant the world to me!

During my junior year, I tried out and made another year on the dance team. I also began attending all the basketball games because my boyfriend, Fred, was a player on the team. Lisa went with me each time, and she started to like one of Fred's friends who was also on the team. Even when they played against our school, El Dorado, we would sit on Valencia's side, as that is where they went to high school.

Both Fred and his friend were seniors. Soon, Lisa and I were spending a lot of our time together cheering them on! We had such a blast watching them show off their athletic skills. All four of us would take off after a weekend game and head down to the beach. We would walk around, each couple going their separate ways. Fred and I had some special, intimate moments together there at the beach, on the sand.

During my junior year, I was also one of the nominees for the Winter Formal Princess. The night of the winter formal, I was dressed in a long white dress with my long blond hair curled perfectly, attending the dance with the "love of my life." Ultimately, I did not win the title, but it was a fun night, and I had been surprised that I was even popular enough to be nominated.

Fred and I also went to the Sadie Hawkins Dance together at Valencia High School, where he went to school. We wore matching plaid shirts and jeans and had a great time laughing and dancing. I do recall one song that was played, "When the Lights Go Down" by Journey. We were slow-dancing and looking into one another's eyes. It was very romantic and meaningful to me.

The last time Fred ever came to my house was on April 30, 1981—when he broke up with me! Just a week or so before, on

April 18, he had told me "I love you" for the first time. I had really fallen for him, and I'd told him that I loved him too. Deep down, half of me had regrets, and half of my thoughts were "take it slow and meaningful." Boy, did I think my life was over when we broke up! We had been dating for seven months. I sat swinging in the hanging chair in my room, crying and looking out the window. I began writing poems, and of course, at that time they were all about Fred, my first love.

Lisa and I often visited late at night at a drive-through donut shop. I so clearly recall Lisa and I munching on donuts—usually three each—sitting low in my green Mustang after midnight, parked down the street from Fred's house. We would watch for him like spies as we waited for him to get home. I think we did this before, during, and after Fred and I were dating. Pretty sneaky, huh?

Also during my junior year, I was introduced to a lady who came to my high school once a week during lunchtime to teach students about Jesus and the Bible. Her name was Nook, and she was from an organization called Campus Crusade for Christ. She began a weekly Bible study at her apartment in Fullerton that Lisa and some other friends from school joined. It was fun, and I learned a lot.

# ≈3≈

# Lost in the Swamp

When I began my senior year in high school, I started hanging out more with a new friend. That was, of course, when she was not busy with a guy she was going out with or we had nothing better to do. I felt kind of alone and needed a friend around, so I took advantage of the times she had free.

You see, this friendship was not a positive influence on me during this time, and continuing to hang out with her led me to pursue unwise choices and in a direction that caused me to fall away from my faith. Dad and Mom had told me—especially Dad—that they did not want me to hang out with her, but I did not respect or listen to their advice. Lisa did not get along with this girl too well, and so she and I did not spend as much time together that school year.

I was not hanging around with my sister Sherrie as much anymore, as she had moved out of the house and was now renting an apartment. Throughout high school, I babysat my other sister, Laura, and my brother, Donald, quite often as Mom began to work outside of the home.

Looking back, the friendship I had begun at the beginning of my senior year had a big impact on my self-esteem. She was a huge influence on my behavior, but unfortunately, this was not in a positive way. We often ditched classes or left the El Dorado campus during assemblies. We snuck out and headed to my green '68 Mustang, which I usually parked across the street.

Many, many times I locked my keys inside the car and would

not realize it until we tried to open the door in a hurry. Since it was an older car, all we had to do was to raise the lock sticking up inside. So off we would go to a neighbor's house, to knock on the door and politely ask for a wire hanger. We then straightened out the hanger, put it through the crack between the window and door, and pulled up the lock. Simple as that!

One particular day when we ditched class, we headed over to McDonald's for some fries and a shake. As we were sitting at a booth, much to our surprise, our school principal and vice principal walked in! They smiled and sat down to join us. Obviously, back to school we went—straight to the office! Other times before and after this day, I forged my mom's signature on a note I had written, to use as an excuse to return to school after ditching.

Another time, this friend and I were cruising the Camelot Golf parking lot, trying to pick up on boys. While the Doors or Rod Stewart blasted from my car's CD player, I switched seats with her, letting her drive my Mustang. On this particular day, we had been drinking, and when my friend got in the driver's seat, she backed right into a parked car. We did not stop but just drove off laughing. Unfortunately, a witness to the accident wrote down my license plate number and put it on the windshield of the car we hit, because later on, my parents received a notice in the mail concerning this issue. I lied and told my parents that I was not aware that this had taken place. They believed me, so they simply paid to have the other car repaired.

More and more bad situations were occurring in my life, causing me to drift further away from my family, and more importantly, from my faith. Most Sundays, I told my parents that I was going to the church service in the evening, but instead I would head over to my new friend's house to do not much of anything. Still, although I drifted away from God that last year of high school, I continued to attend Campus by the Sea in Catalina each summer. My main goal at Bible camp, though, was mostly centered on finding a new boyfriend. That did not happen!

During the summer, my parents went to our cabin in Big Bear for a holiday weekend with my sister Laura and brother, Donald. That meant I was home alone all weekend, and in my senior year I decided to throw a party on the Sunday afternoon when my family was gone. Lisa and I went around the neighborhood to inform those nearby about the party, so I would not have to worry about the police being called. I also let them know a band would be playing.

I was accepted at the University of California in San Diego, or UCSD, and I packed my belongings and headed off to college after high school to begin a new life. My major was in child psychology; I wanted to become a child psychologist in order to help abused children.

I moved into a dorm at Muir College that was one of three others on campus. My dorm room was in Tioga Hall, and my roommate's name was Krysten. She was genuinely nice—petite and funny—though kind of shy. When she partied, though, she became a lot more open and silly. I came to find out that Muir College was well-known as the "party place" on campus.

On each floor of the dorms, one side was for the guys and the opposite was for us girls. Krysten and I lived on the second floor, which was named the Roaring 20s. There were continuous kegs of beer, parties, bongs with pot, and spoon games for shots of tequila. Of course, some studying also took place, after which I caught up on sleep, recovered from my hangover, and then returned to my weekly party habits.

During my first year of college, I did try hard in my work habits with school, besides going to all the parties. I often visited Lisa, who now lived in Laguna Beach and attended San Diego State University. On occasional weekends, I would stay with her or she would come down to San Diego to hit the parties with me around campus, which usually were every weekend. When we stayed together, we often would go late after partying to pick up some frozen yogurt. I also did this with dorm friends, during late breaks from studying, and this is when my addiction to frozen yogurt began!

At the beginning of my freshman year, I met a guy at one of the parties on campus. He also was attending UCSD and lived in La Jolla. He had blue eyes and wavy blond hair. At our first party in the dorms, I noticed how cute he was. When we spoke to each other, I saw that he had a darling smile. Later, I would spot him hanging out with friends in the dorms, in between classes, or at parties nearby. We mostly got together to socialize after a few drinks during or after parties. However, I learned that he had an "off and on" girlfriend from high school who was a year younger than him, and this would often interfere with any plans that we made.

Boy, did I gain a lot of weight during my time away at college, as I was eating three meals a day in the cafeteria, which my parents were paying for, along with my tuition, gas, books, and entertainment. I had it all! But also adding to the weight was all the alcohol I had been consuming, which had started in my later years of high school.

During the time I was seeing this new cute guy from La Jolla, Lisa and I joined him and his best friend, Andy, on an excursion to Rosarito Beach in Mexico. Many other kids crammed into Andy's long station wagon for the cruise over the border. It was a weekend night, so off we went to party, driving in a car that was too full for us to put on seat belts. On this night, Andy was introduced to Lisa. I do not remember if it was Lisa and I who did the planning for the trip, or if it was the boys.

For Andy and Lisa, it seemed like "love at first sight"! I can still picture us sitting in a large group at a long table, each of us with a drink, celebrating who knows what, simply happy to be together and party. Andy and Lisa were sitting at the end of the table across from each other, talking the night away. They began dating each other soon after, and from then on they could not stand to be apart. Years later, they got married.

When Lisa came to visit UCSD, we often would meet up with the guy I liked, along with Andy and some other friends, to hang out and to go to parties. We would often go to a hole-in-the-wall Mexican restaurant in Del Mar. Usually, it was just friends from my dorm or the bigger gang, including Andy and Lisa. When we dined at this place, my friend from the dorm would often bring her boyfriend with her as well. He was not very social, but even though no one really cared for him, we welcomed him anyway and took advantage of the fact that he was twenty-one and could legally order drinks for us.

This guy would order a pitcher of lemonade margaritas, and everyone else at the table ordered glasses of water. We then gracefully guzzled down our waters and took turns passing the pitcher around, filling up our empty glasses with the margarita mix. He would continuously reorder a full pitcher, and then the passing process continued going around again and again and again! Eventually we would leave the small restaurant full of burritos and margaritas.

As the school year came to an end, my La Jolla boyfriend got back together with his old girlfriend, our dorm friends went their separate ways, and I packed my belongings and headed home.

I had decided to attend summer school at UCSD, yet I still was able to take a short break before moving into an apartment at the other end of campus. I was rooming with Julie from the dorms, along with two other girls we had briefly met from school. My brother, Donald, came to visit me for a weekend, and we hung out at the beach. He often wrote me short notes with little drawings, usually of the crabs at the beach. I think he was only around eight years old at the time.

When summer school ended, I returned home and hung out mostly with my good ol' friend, the girl I had mentioned who had caused me to drift in the wrong direction during my last year of high school. During that summer, she introduced me to a U.S. Marine she had started dating. I would often go with them to Camp Pendleton, where he was stationed and hang out with all the guys. I met many marines—who, by the way, were very flirtatious, further contributing to the wrong choices I was making in my life. I, of course, believed many of them were interested in me.

This all took place not long before I headed into my sophomore year, and my ambition and enthusiasm for studying decreased quite a bit. I began studying less, partying more, going home every weekend from school to see my "friend," and putting a lot less effort in trying to learn anything at all.

During the beginning of my sophomore year at UCSD, I met some more marines at Camp Pendleton. Soon school meant nothing to me. I ended up receiving a D in Psychology, so I decided to change my major at the semester break. My new major was Child Development.

One of the marines I'd met caught my attention with his joking and his accent. I invited him and his friends to attend some of the dorm parties at UCSD, where we enjoyed the free kegs of beer. This marine and I began to like one another toward the end of February during my sophomore year, and we began dating. I drove to meet him a lot in Oceanside, where he lived. At times, he would borrow a motorcycle or hitch a ride to come to my dorm room and stay overnight. Mostly, though, I was the one who was always driving to see him.

Obviously, driving, partying, and dating took up much of my time—and my dedication to school and my future goals steadily decreased. But not long after we had started dating, I discovered that this marine just so happened to be engaged to a much older single lady with two kids, whom he knew from his distant home-town. I met her when she arrived in San Diego to try to work things out between the two of them. Of course, he told me he was breaking things off with this woman, and of course, I believed every word he said. Shortly after, this man, who was a year younger than me, proposed to me, after I had met him just a few months before.

The evening I got engaged, we were at his apartment. We sat down to eat dinner and share a large bottle of red wine, and during the meal, he took out the ring and asked me if I would marry him. Marriage to a guy in the U.S. Marines! Wow! This was so much more important to me than any of my goals associated with UCSD.

I said yes, and my sophomore year continued. I think it was the following weekend that I brought him home to tell my family. They were happy to hear the news and congratulated us. On Sunday, my fiancé, dressed in his marine attire, and I attended St. Joseph's church with my family, before we headed back to San Diego.

Next, his parents came to California to visit their only child and meet their new future daughter-in-law. His parents had a similar personality as their spoiled son. They drank alcohol and laughed as they partied along with us. As we drove back from San Diego, near Mission Bay, my new fiancé was driving my Mustang, while his parents were in the back seat, and we were all drinking beer in the car. We had to make sure we kept the drinks out of sight so the police would not see us drinking and driving.

My fiancé and I happily planned a wedding date for a few months away, in September of the same year, 1984. Lisa, who now had moved closer to her school, SDSU, threw me a bridal shower at her home and invited my college friends before school was out. It was a happy time celebrating, and I was content with my plans to become a beautiful bride.

Soon after all of these events, he and I headed to Big Bear, to my parents' cabin, to stay for the Memorial Day weekend. We had made plans to meet them there and spend the weekend with them along with Laura and Donald. My parents were going to give us some of the furniture at the cabin to take back to his apartment in Oceanside. We were planning on living together there after we were married, which is what we told my parents. I had told them that I wanted to spend the remainder of the summer in La Jolla and take summer school classes. But what we were really planning to do was to move in together when we returned from Big Bear. I was catapulting fast into my future ahead plans, and I barely noticed that I was leaving behind my independence and any plans for my education.

# ≈4≈

## Plans That Didn't

The plans I had been making never took place—as God had other plans for my life instead. The last thing I remember was that we both were leaving in my Mustang, heading to Big Bear. We left La Jolla, but then we stopped at a Jack in the Box before reaching Carlsbad. I was driving, and after we pulled into the parking lot of the restaurant, he opened the trunk, pulled out a small container of whiskey, and chugged some down. I did not drink any alcohol, but instead I bought a Diet Coke to take with me on the road. After that, everything is a huge blur!

*"For I know the plans I have for you," declares the Lord, "plans to prosper you and not to harm you, plans to give you hope and a future"* (Jeremiah 29:11).

The next several paragraphs are filled with information about the incident that took place next. This occurred thirty-five years ago, and I was told what happened—I have no personal recollection of the details.

I was involved in a serious automobile accident on May 24, 1984, while coming off the freeway onto Central Avenue, in Redlands, California. There was no signal there, just a stop sign. I pulled out from the off-ramp in my Mustang and was immediately hit by a large van coming from the other direction. One witness told the police that the man driving the van was not paying attention to the road, as he was apparently reading a map.

At that time, there was no law that required seat belts, so of course, my fiancé and I did not have them on. He saw the van approaching and said something, but it was too late. He was holding on, so he just tore a few ligaments in his leg. I, on the other hand, took a lot more of the impact in this accident, both physically and emotionally, and later in the future, I came to realize I had been affected spiritually as well.

Upon impact, my head hit the dashboard as I swung forward. I fell to the right and broke some ribs when my body hit the stick shift; this was not noticed until weeks later.

I was unconscious, and paramedics rushed me to Loma Linda Hospital in an ambulance. My favorite car, which I had named "Astro," was totaled and later towed to my parents' home in Placentia. My parents were called; they were already at the cabin in Big Bear. They rushed down the winding mountain road to Loma Linda Hospital.

I was in a coma, but immediately I was rushed into surgery, as I had fractured my skull and had severe head trauma. The doctors told my parents they did not know whether or not I would make it through the surgery. If I did recover, they said, I would most likely remain a vegetable for the rest of my life, due to the damage my brain had sustained from the impact.

My parents borrowed a motor home that they could park in the hospital's parking lot so they could stay as near to me as possible. My dad had to continue working whenever he could, as he had owned a steel company since 1975. While I was in the coma, I had a grand mal seizure. To try to prevent more seizures from occurring, I was put on phenobarbital. Many, many relatives and friends began praying for my recovery, and my mother was continually by my side.

Lisa came to visit me in the hospital. She was the "friend" connection, trying to reach me at some level while I was in the coma. She babbled on and on, laughed, joked around, and I am sure, gossiped here and there too. She wanted to talk to me in the same way we had chatted for so many years, hanging out together or at sleepovers. Lisa told me about this recently; she said that her goal was "reach into me and pull me back to Lisa's way."

On the ninth day of my coma, Lisa was by my side, talking to me and reading from a magazine, which she often brought to share with me. I suddenly squeezed her hand and fluttered my eyes! I had not done this before since I'd been in the coma. But on that day, I soon began moving my bent legs from side to side. Lisa remembered how I would often lie in this position in bed when we had attended sleepovers together in the past. Wow!

Everyone thought things were beginning to change for me, and the doctors said this could be a sign that I might soon be coming out of the coma. On the tenth day of the coma, as my dad was standing next to my hospital bed, I opened my eyes, saw him, and said, "Shave your beard!" He went right away and shaved it with a smile, as those were the first words I had spoken after I came out of the coma. The doctors and nurses told my parents this was the beginning of my recovery and remarked that all of the prayers had played a large part in the miracle that was taking place.

At the beginning of my fourth week in the hospital, I began to regain my memory little by little. Thus, the following memories are those that I recall on my own, regarding my time in the hospital after I awoke from the coma.

I was sitting at the end of my bed when the nurse began to remove the stitches from the left side of my head. Three weeks after the first surgery, the surgeons replaced the part of my skull that had initially been removed due to swelling and pressure of my brain against the skull that took place during the first surgery. Therefore, my full head of hair had been shaved twice, although I only recall it happening the second time. When my hair was shaved, I saw a large scar on the left side of my head. It pretty much reached from the top of my ear to the side edge of my forehead, in a C shape. The scar was there for good. The right side of my body was paralyzed, and when I went to physical therapy, I would try to walk along two raised bars that I tightly held with both hands.

A yellow slip of paper was placed by my bed, with the names of my family and friends: Mom, Dad, Sherrie, Pat, Lisa, Donald, and the guy I was in love with. It came in handy when someone would come to visit me—I could look at the paper to remember their names. I knew who they were, but I could not remember their name. This thinking process issue was due to my lack of short-term memory caused by the injury on the left side of my brain. While I stayed at Loma Linda, I began speech therapy as well.

After four weeks, I was transferred to St. Jude's Hospital in Fullerton, California, to undergo speech, occupational, and physical therapy. In occupational therapy, I made a ceramic hot pad, which I still have and sometimes use today. I was also retaught how to write out a personal check. I had forgotten so many little actions that we all take for granted. In physical therapy, I had to continually work on my right side, while rebuilding my overall strength.

I remained as a patient at St. Jude's for three more weeks followed by speech therapy for a year after I was finally released. The total time I spent in both hospitals was seven long weeks. I continued seeing the same therapist as an outpatient, which worked out well. My mom drove me to therapy three times a week. The little I remember of it was that the therapist and I would sit across from each other as she asked me simple questions.

Many years later, I looked at all the paperwork my parents kept from the accident, including some of my responses during speech therapy. When I was asked, "What did you have for lunch today?" I once answered, "Knott's Berry Farm, Very Berry." I might have known the answer, but due to the loss of my short-term memory, I had a hard time answering questions correctly. It took dedicated time, but I made tremendous progress in a year.

I was twenty years old, and I had been living on my own for almost two years while attending UCSD. Now my life had changed tremendously! I needed to be with at least one of my parents, constantly, for three months after being discharged from the hospital. My driver's license was taken away for a year after my accident due to the seizure I'd had. I had to wait and then re-take the behind-the-wheel driving test. This was definitely a hard time for me to adjust to.

Boy, those few months were not very enjoyable. I hated being Mom's little girl all over again. I was out shopping with Mom one day at Mervyn's, and a few boys started staring at me, laughing and whispering. They made a comment about my shaved head and the noticeable scar on my scalp. They spoke these exact words: "What are you, a punk rocker? Hahaha!" Furious, I responded, "No! I was in a serious automobile accident!" They felt awful and apologized before hurrying away.

You may have been wondering what happened to my fiancé. I don't recall seeing him much, maybe once or twice while I was in the hospital. I clearly do know of my last visit with him at my home. He came over on a Saturday to see me and hang out; he drove up on a motorcycle he borrowed from a friend at Camp Pendleton. No one was at home besides me except my sister Laura and my mom. She was upstairs in the attic, cleaning or sorting through stuff.

My fiancé and I were sitting on the couch in the family room watching *Gilligan's Island*. I vaguely remember him caressing me, then he took my hand and guided me into the office, next to the family room. My mother came down the stairs and walked by the office, heading to the garage. When she saw him, she demanded loudly that he leave!

Obviously, I was at the beginning stages of recovery from the brain trauma caused by my accident, so my actions, mental processing, and logic were not in the normal range. I was yelling for him, screaming, crying, and begging him not to leave, or if he did, to take me with him. He said that he could not, and off he drove on the motorcycle back to Camp Pendleton. I was overwhelmed by all that was happening, but I would soon learn information that I really did not want to hear.

I went upstairs to my room. I was crying and swinging in my hanging chair, looking out the sliding glass door. Pat and Sherrie came from Riverside, where they lived, to talk to me later that afternoon. When they arrived, I ran out to them, crying, hoping they would be on my side and understand what had happened. Sherrie held me tight as Pat began to tell me something that I did not want to hear or accept.

While I was in the hospital, my fiancé was flirting with my cousin. Pat had decided to take him to a local bar one night, to take a break from the hospital and get a drink. He also did this to keep an eye on him and determine what type of guy my future husband really was. Sure enough, Pat told me that my fiancé had tried to pick up other girls at the bar, even as I lay critically ill in the hospital. This was not what I had expected or wanted to hear at this time in my life.

I was heartbroken. I specifically remember sitting at the kitchen table while Mom was cooking dinner and peeling potatoes, and I sadly said, "I just want to die!" I put my head down on the table in my arms and sobbed.

I tried to talk with this man who had wrapped me around his finger. I even wrote him letters, telling him I would forgive him. But never again did I see his face or hear from him. My life felt as if I had nothing ahead to work for, and I wanted to end it.

# ~5~

# A Chance for My Future

Three months after my accident, I was able to go out with a friend. I finally had achieved some independence from my parents, although Mom and Dad watched over me like a hawk when they were around. They cared deeply for me and were concerned for my safety and healing.

Lisa and I began to go out again to El Torito, where we ate chips and salsa and danced our hearts away. Back then, they had a large dance floor where we would often hang out, after we turned eighteen years old. My hair had grown out a bit, but you could still see the large scar on the side of my head. Also, after the accident, I was not able to hear as well out of my right ear, due to the brain injury on the left side of my head, and I was unable to use my right ear to listen on the phone ever again. The words would sound blurry, as if they were an echo.

Another part of my newfound independence was substituting at George Key School, located up the street, next to Golden Elementary. George Key had been established by the county to educate mentally and physically disabled students from the ages of three through twenty-two. This was where my sister Laura went to school.

I could work as an instructional aide, as I was now able to speak clearly and follow instructions, but I had a hard time remembering if too much information was given at one time. The job fit into my ability category because the work was basic and with students who had special needs, so the aides did not need to have a college degree. Not long after I began substituting, I was hired, and I continued working there for five more years.

One of the aides working in Laura's class was Mary. After I got to know her, she wanted to set me up with her brother. She showed me his picture and told me how nice he was. His name was Norm, and he lived in Downey. I finally decided to go on a blind date with him to Mimi's Café for breakfast. We also went bowling.

Our blind date took place in December 1984. During breakfast at Mimi's, Norm and I spoke about our past engagement relationships. We talked on and on about our lives, opening our hearts to one another even though we were almost strangers. We each shared the mistakes we had made in the past. Norm had lived with his fiancée, and I was pretty much living with mine either at my dorm room or in Oceanside.

Since my accident, I had lost thirty-five pounds! I swam laps in my parents' pool almost every day. Another reason I lost so much weight was because I could no longer drink alcohol, as I had regularly done in the past, both during high school and at UCSD. Also, I was not eating at the school cafeteria three times a day and snacking all the time in between. Instead, I was eating my mom's delicious, home-cooked meals.

I did see Norm again after our first date. Even though conversation was easy between us, I was not attracted to him physically. His clothes were out of fashion, and he just did not seem like my type. Later on, Norm would call me, hoping to come visit, but I would say to my dad, "Tell him I'm not here." I had no interest in dating again.

However, Norm was persistent—he even delivered a balloon bouquet to my workplace on my twenty-first birthday in April and came by my house when my parents had family over to celebrate. I figured he finally got the hint that I was not interested in him when he stopped calling me.

Not long before my birthday, my doctor decided to take me off phenobarbital, my seizure medication. I had been taking it for almost a year, with no signs of seizure episodes. The doctor let me know that since I was going off the medication, I could now drink alcohol, in small amounts.

To celebrate, Lisa and I went to party at El Torito, where we drank beer and hit the dance floor. I remember wearing jeans, a hot-pink shirt, and white boots. While there, we bumped into a guy whom I had thought was cute in my senior year in high school; he went to Valencia. We talked for a bit and danced while another guy who was with him flirted with Lisa.

In June that year, I took the behind-the-wheel driving test to get my license back. It had been a year, and I was excited to be able to drive again. I remember anxiously sitting in the car, ready to begin the testing. Thankfully, I passed, and my license was renewed. Yahoo! However, I was told I was only allowed to drive cars with mirrors on both the right side and the left side of the vehicle. Because of nerve damage caused by the accident, I no longer had peripheral vision.

I was able to drink alcohol again, and I'd gotten my driver's license back. My hair was also long enough for me to get a perm at the hair salon. I had made so much progress, but I still had a long journey ahead of me.

Around this time, I went to see a neurologist whom I had previously seen at St. Jude's. He recently had done an MRI scan of my brain, a year after the accident. As I sat there in his office, he informed me of the results, as well as the long-term consequences. I would likely never return to college to pursue my degree in child development. Because my accident had injured the left side of my brain, my memory had been permanently affected. I could retain small amounts of information, but trying to store too much at one time in my brain would be too overwhelming. The doctor told me I could try taking one class, something with information that was familiar to me, and see how it went, but he wasn't optimistic. Wow! I was heartbroken as it seemed my dreams were never going to come true.

In late June, as I was talking to my uncle on the phone at home, I began to rattle on, babbling words in a conversation that did not make any sense at all. The next thing I knew, I was waking up in a hospital room at St. Jude's again. I had had another grand mal seizure as I was talking on the phone. Although the doctor put me back on phenobarbital, thankfully I was allowed to continue driving. The dosage made me tired, and again I returned to the recovery process.

A few weeks after I left the hospital, Norm called me out of the blue. We had not spoken since my birthday, so I assumed he was calling to see how I was feeling after the seizure. I had missed a few days of work, and I thought his sister Mary had told him what happened. Norm told me he had not heard about this, but he just had been thinking of me and wanted to see how I was doing. When he asked if I would like to get together again, I said yes.

Norm came to pick me up on July 14, and we spent the day in Long Beach at the Queen Mary. We hung out, walked around the ship, and took some crazy, but silly pictures. Later, as we were eating at a restaurant, Norm stood up from the table, got down on one knee, pointed to his left ring finger, and said, "Look, Neil Diamond." It was a joke. Hahaha!

Yes, it was a weird joke to tell on our second date, but I laughed. We both were pretty much on the same page, so I thought I might give the relationship a try. Why not? We began seeing each other on a regular basis, and that was the first of many, many off the wall jokes Norm would tell me.

Norm worked at Mechanical Drives in Los Angeles, and he lived in Downey. It was a long drive for him to take me out to dinner, but I guess I was worth the drive! He later told me that on the way home, he would often have to pull over to buy some sugary donuts and caffeinated coffee to stay awake.

At the start of our dating relationship, we planned on going to a Christian dance event together. Well, when he came to pick me up, I could not believe what he was wearing! He had on a white, long-sleeved polyester shirt and black silk pants. *Oh my gosh, I have to be seen in public with him dressed like this!* was what I was thinking. We did have a fairly good time, even though he told me he did not really know how to dance. This was true! After we started dating, I made it a point to go through his closet of clothes and toss out the most embarrassing outfits—and then we went on a shopping spree.

Norm's parents had separated many times as he was growing up, and at one point, his mom had a nervous breakdown and was admitted to the hospital. At this time, Norm and his two younger brothers were placed in foster homes. Because Norm and one of his brothers were close in age, they were placed together in a home in Long Beach for almost two years.

Their foster family brought the boys each week to a Christian church, which made a huge impact on Norm at that time in his life. When his mother, Cathy, was well again and out of the hospital, Norm's father got back together with her, Norm, and both of his brothers. At that time, Norm was in junior high. His three older sisters were out on their own or married when his parents had separated. Norm had had a beautiful life with his foster parents, and he wished, at times, he could have continued living with them as he grew up.

Norm went to Huntington High School, the same school my dad had graduated from. Norm graduated at the age of seventeen by taking a proficiency exam with a hundred other students. Only five students passed, and he was one of them. He then began his future career at Mechanical Drive's, starting off working in the warehouse.

After Norm and his fiancé broke up, his older sister Norma brought him to a Calvary church. That day, he committed himself to the Lord, and he never strayed from his faith, beliefs, and lifestyle. When I met him, he had just turned twenty-three years old. At work, he had advanced from the warehouse to become an inside sales manager. He was very independent, yet he also wanted to help his parents, and so he let them move in with him. The following is a verse from the Bible that Norm often thought of and shared:

> *Honor your father and your mother, so that you may live long in the land the Lord your God is giving you* (Exodus 20:12).

Norm encouraged me to sign up for a class at Cal State Fullerton to see how I would do in remembering the information I learned. I enrolled in a class in psychology or child development. I had been in the class for about three weeks, when I started studying for a test coming up and I realized the doctor was right. I could not process new information and be able to remember it without having the information in front of me to read and be reminded of.

Yes, my life had changed, and my future would begin a new chapter. I had been hired at George Key School for a full-time position as an instructional aide a few months before. Norm continued to uplift my spirits and often reminded me of the impact I was making on the special needs children I worked with. He encouraged me along the journey, one step at a time, and accepted me for who I was. He did not judge me because of my faulty intellect.

# ≈6≈

# "Suzy, Will You Marry Me?"

I clearly recall going to a store in downtown Fullerton at the Orange Fair Mall. It was called S&H Green Stamps. Here, you would place your order of merchandise, and the product would come from the back, down a conveyor belt, and then be purchased with green stamps. Norm and I were there for a very important reason—to look at wedding rings! Yes, it was true. We had been dating only since July 14, but on October 19, 1985, we got engaged!

However, before Norm proposed to me, he had a conversation with my dad in our dining room, in which he asked for Dad's permission to marry me. Of course, my dad said yes, and we made plans to head to Laguna Beach on October 19.

We walked past some rocks and found a location in a pretty cove, then rolled open a sleeping bag to rest on the sand. We sat down with our tortilla chips, salsa, and sparkling apple cider, enjoying the beautiful sight of the water hitting the rocks on the shore. I had told Norm that I did not want his proposal to be a surprise. I wanted to help plan it out, and so I thought things were going accordingly.

Well, leave it to Norm to surprise me! He was following the plans I had made for my "dream come true" proposal. He knelt next to a rock in front of me and began to propose, but then he suddenly stopped! "Oops!" he said. "I left the ring in the car." He then got up and began to turn away, as if he was heading to the parking lot, while he pulled the ring out of his sock without me noticing. Then Norm quickly said, "Suzy, will you marry me?" Sneaky, sneaky, sneaky! Of course, I replied yes.

A month later, we celebrated Pat and Sherrie's wedding. She was pregnant, but she still wanted to wear our mom's wedding dress. Since Mom only weighed 98 pounds when our parents got married, the dress had to be altered to fit her. Their outdoor wedding was beautiful. As Norm and I danced at the reception, I dreamed of our own wedding. I could not wait for this time to be ours the following year. I also happily caught the bridal bouquet!

Around this time in my life, I became a bit of a TV game show "star." I went along with Sherrie and two other ladies to try out for *The Price Is Right*. Sherrie was quite noticeably pregnant at the time. As we went up in groups of four people, we each had a short interview with a lady who would then choose the contestants. When my turn came, I was loud and spontaneous when I told her my name and age. I then proceeded to tap Sherrie's tummy and told her how I could not wait to be a proud aunt in a few months. I had a huge smile on my face.

Well, that did it. When the show went on air, they announced, "Suzanne Palmer, come on down! You're the next contestant on *The Price Is Right*!" I was the fourth one called down in the first row of the beginning contestants. Boy, was I nervous!

I only recall looking back one time at Sherrie in the audience for help in guessing the price of the merchandise shown. We were each told backstage before the show that we were not to look toward the audience for help in pricing the items onstage. I pretty much "went by the rules in the book" as I had done in most of my younger years.

I never once quoted the closest price, but I brought home some handy dandy consolation prizes. I received a tabletop lamp that was in the shape of a mushroom, about thirty boxes of Success Rice, and plenty of large boxes of Junior Mints. Norm was working when the show aired on TV, so he recorded it. Yes, I still do have that exciting tape of when I was a "short-term" celebrity… Haha!

Norm and I set our big day for May 31, 1986. Sherrie was to be my matron of honor, I had asked Lisa to be maid of honor, and my bridesmaids were Norm's two older sisters, Mary and Norma. Our flower girls were my sister Laura and Laurie, whom I had babysat many years before. We also asked Mary's son to be our ring bearer.

During our engagement, Norm, my parents, and I had to complete a deposition with my lawyer concerning the accident. The attorney of the person who hit my car was also present. A statement was taken from both parties, and the information led to a settlement in my favor. I carried home $12,000 and put it in the bank right away.

To me, the wedding was a new start after a long recovery. Yes, I had recovered from a major accident, healed from several surgeries, and was left with a large scar on the left side of my head. No hair ever grew back over my scar, but it was hidden as the rest of my hair slowly covered it. Although the scar eventually was not noticeable physically, mentally the accident affected me for the rest of my life, much more than any amount of money could compensate for.

The right side of my body was physically affected, as I mentioned previously. My right arm and leg had weakness, and my right leg would also become sore just by walking or standing too much. Driving in traffic, continually pressing on the brake, would be quite painful in my right shin and foot.

Another issue that permanently affected my brain is my memory. My mind drifts at times, and it is hard to think of a certain word or remember the meanings of words I knew before the accident. I often can come up with the first letter of a word, but I can't finish the thought process to come up with the whole word. When I ask the meaning of a word, or the name of something, I often forget it right after I am told. I had to start writing things down to remember them, and so taking notes became my new habit.

Norm had become my best friend! He built up my self-esteem and assured me of my true value in life and the importance of who I was. He encouraged me through difficult times and when I often had a fear of confrontation. He helped me work on becoming a strong individual who had qualities that God wanted me to share. I do not believe I would be where I am today if it had not been for Norm's faith and strength.

I have learned more about spiritual guidance and understanding using the word "discernment"—which means to show good judgment. As I will explain, you will see how both Norm and certain books I read were stepping-stones for my future gain of wisdom and discernment through knowledge and experience. We proceeded together with our future goals and enjoyed one another's company along the way.

*And this is my prayer: that your love may abound more and more in knowledge and depth of insight, so that you may be able to discern what is best and may be pure and blameless for the day of Christ* (Philippians 1:9–10).

On March 21, 1986, Sherrie gave birth to Christopher, my first nephew, who had probably gotten me on *The Price Is Right*. Norm and I dreamed and discussed our future family. We surely would want to have children one day. He brought me over to introduce me to his foster parents one day, after we rode our bikes at El Dorado Park in Long Beach.

Time passed quickly while planning our wedding, and we had to make sure Mom's wedding dress was altered once again for me, after Sherrie's wedding. Yes, I too wanted to wear this old-fashioned wedding dress. It had long, lacy sleeves and buttons up the lower part of each arm, flowery lace all over, and many consecutive buttons from the neck to below the waist in the back. It also had a large hoop skirt that flared out from the dress. It was beautiful, and I felt like a princess when I wore it.

Mom was very busy planning all the details and making the reservations before our important date arrived. The date grew closer, and my bridal showers began. The Junior Mints that I had received from the game show were used as shower mints. We received so many nice gifts from special people to decorate our new home and share with my future husband, Norm!

Speaking of our new home, one month before we were married, Norm moved into our first apartment, one we had chosen in Placentia. The apartment complex was called The Streams. Ours was a two-story, studio apartment with a loft above, which would be our bedroom. In the family room, there was a sliding door that led to a small patio with a flowing stream running next to it.

We had our rehearsal dinner at Don Jose's in the banquet room at the back of the restaurant. Before the dinner took place, though, we all met at St. Joseph's church to rehearse. The wedding party proceeded down the aisle in groups of two, followed by the flower girls and the ring bearer. My dad then walked me to the front of the church to greet Norm. We practiced our wedding vows and left there with large smiles, so excited and happy. Lisa spent the night with me before the wedding, and we went out to dance and splurged on chips and salsa together, our usual routine.

May 31, 1986—our big day—had finally arrived! I got dressed in my parent's bedroom, while the photographer was there shooting many photos. Our wedding began at noon, yet we were all up early to get ourselves looking beautiful. Sherrie, Laura, Lisa, and my mom were there with me. My hair was curled and styled with lots of hairspray. When I was ready, I went to the top of the staircase in my mom's beautiful wedding gown and looked down the steps at everyone below. My Aunt Carolyn also had joined the ladies and the photographer as he was taking photos of me going down the staircase.

Lisa then took my hand and led me to the front door. Sitting in the cul-de-sac next to the curb, I was a shocked to see a white Rolls-Royce waiting to drive me off for my dream day ahead. I was surprised, but I had said in the past, as well as written it in my high school yearbook, that one day I would own a convertible Rolls-Royce! Of course, I did not own the car and it wasn't a convertible, which would have messed up my hairdo anyway, but who cares? I could not believe my eyes! I hugged Lisa tightly and began to get tears, but I suddenly stopped them so my makeup would not be messed up.

After Norm kissed me at the end of the ceremony, we turned around and threw up our hands together, with the bouquet in my right hand. We stood out back at the church and greeted those who attended, including a few of my dorm friends from college. We then proceeded to Alta Vista Country Club, where our reception took place.

Special moments from the reception that I hold dear to my heart included when Norm and I toasted, when Chuck and Lisa gave meaningful messages, our first dance, cutting the layered cake with a Precious Moments figurine cake topper, and dancing the night away.

At the end, I threw the bouquet, and then Norm, smiling with a romantic look on his face, peeled the blue garter off my leg. He then tossed it, and I think Donald, my younger brother who was only eleven years old, caught it. Hahaha! We then drove off in our small white Toyota sedan, decorated with a "Just Married" sign on the back window.

We headed to Laguna in the evening and spent the first night in our honeymoon suite at Riviera Laguna. The hotel was painted a light-blue sea color, and our window overlooked the ocean. I put on my white lacy negligee, which I had received at one of my showers as a gift from Lisa. In fact, I still have that negligee in my dresser drawer. Looking out onto the ocean, our night drifted away, both of us tired yet full of romance.

The romance continued for a few more days as we woke up early the next morning and headed to San Diego for the remaining part of our honeymoon. We first had breakfast at this cute little restaurant in Laguna, on the corner where the sand came to an end and the shopping stores and restaurants began. It was called Greeter's Corner Café. We sat on the outdoor patio, overlooking the water. Breakfast was Norm's favorite meal of the day. He would often order the combo plate at restaurants, which usually included two eggs over-easy, bacon, potatoes with grilled onions, toast or biscuits, and gravy.

Leaving Laguna, we stopped off in San Juan Capistrano to go to church at the mission. After the service, we walked around the mission inn, fed the swallows, and tossed a few coins in the large water fountain in the courtyard. Next, we headed for Vacation Village, where we stayed for a couple of nights. Our backyard patio was on the sand, followed by the water of Mission Bay. It had beautiful scenery, especially at night! We had our first dinner delivered to our room, Norm wearing his gray sweatpants and I had on my fancy, silk pajamas.

The following days, we flew kites, went to Sea World, and rented a cart to pedal around in. On the last morning, Norm and I ate our breakfast, out the sliding door of our room, at the table pulled out onto the sand. We went by my parents' house on the way home to finish opening gifts and pack them up to take to our new home. I sat on Norm's lap and read to my family from our journal where we had written about our honeymoon adventures.

# ≈7≈

# Sharing Faith

Now, being a newly married couple, begins another chapter, or stepping-stone, in my future. I knew one of the top things on my mind, and I had mentioned it to Norm beforehand. I wanted to cook some hearty casseroles for him to put on some weight. He surely needed to gain weight, because when we met and were married, he only weighed 122 pounds.

Our first year was full of traveling to different places. We flew to Texas to visit Norm's grandparents in Fort Worth, and then we drove to Houston to stay with my Great-great-great-Aunt Loraine, as she liked me to exaggerate the word great. Around Christmastime, we drove to Solvang and brought a tandem bicycle that we had purchased for our Christmas gift. We enjoyed looking at all the beautiful Christmas lights outdoors, ate at the bakeries, and rode our tandem along a bike path while enjoying the scenery.

In December, Norm was offered a different job. He had been wanting to become an outside salesman and was offered something different, so he took the job and only stayed there for about one year. He then became a happier outside salesman at Southwest Controls in Chino, and he enjoyed it, advancing with his career.

For our first anniversary, Norm and I traveled on the Catalina Express and spent a week in Catalina. We went snorkeling and saw many beautiful fish and took photos with an underwater camera. We also went on a submarine while looking through a glass-bottom boat to see nature underwater. Before heading back to the ship, we stopped off at a stand to search for and pull up clam shells for our first two pearls. Those special two pearls were put into a ring Norm had made for me, which I still wear today.

We began to enjoy bike riding more and more on the tandem bike. It was fun riding together, and Christopher, my nephew, was our first baby passenger. After one year of being married, we moved to a condominium complex and rented a one-story, two-bedroom condo. We still lived in Placentia, and it was even closer to my parents' home. It was also right across the street from my work at George Key School.

I began to lose interest in attending church each week as we were still going to St. Joseph's. Norm would routinely go, and he would continue to ask me to go along too, but I would often refuse. I believe Norm was living out what I came to find out much later was his favorite Bible verse:

*I pray that your partnership with us in the faith may be effective in deepening your understanding of every good thing we share for the sake of Christ* (Philemon 1:6).

We lived on Micmac for about a year, and Norm and I made many memories together during this time. When riding on the tandem together, we often stopped off at Heidi's Frozen Yogurt. This is where I became addicted to my daily habit of taking a frozen yogurt to work each day for lunch. We also enjoyed going out every Friday night for dinner at a Mexican restaurant.

We went to parks together, walking around and enjoying one another's company. One time, we were parked at Tri-City Park, lying in the back of his truck overlooking the lake. He leaned over to kiss me and said, "I love you, Katie." I was so upset, but right away he caught himself, and I never heard that name again. You see, Katie had been his fiancée before we had met!

During our third year of marriage, we bought a two-story condominium at the other end of the same complex in Placentia. It was on a street called Chickasaw. Norm sweetly carried me in his arms over the front threshold of the first home we had purchased.

After a few months went by, we found out I was pregnant and would be due close to our third anniversary. I had an MRI done just to see if there was any way I could, while pregnant, stop my seizure medication. There were some chances of various side effects that could occur with the baby, yet I was unable to stop my medication.

I became remarkably busy sewing a mattress cover for the crib and some matching cushions for a rocking chair to reupholster. The material was adorable, with elephants in pastel baby colors all over it. Norm put up wallpaper all over the room with similar baby-colored thin stripes. The future baby room was now ready and waiting as we were coming up close to my delivery date.

Norm and I decided to begin looking around for a new church in which we could raise our future family. When we made this change, I began to be more devoted in following the path the Lord was leading me, and I attended church with my husband each week.

*Start children off on the way they should go, and even when they are old they will not turn from it* (Proverbs 22:6).

We first tried out The Vineyard in Anaheim. When we began attending, the church was quite small and located in an industrial building. Inside, there were many folding chairs for guests to sit in and worship. We also became involved in a Bible study group there and met with them once a week.

A month before my due date, I quit my job, where I had been working for five years. Norm had strongly declared that he did not want me to work when we had children. He wanted me to be a stay-at-home mom, and if we had to, we would live in a tent to be able to afford it! Yes, those were his exact words thirty years ago.

We celebrated our third anniversary on May 31, but there was still no baby. After being two weeks overdue, I was induced at Kaiser Hospital. We had our first baby, a girl, Nichole Michelle, with her middle name the same as mine, on June 5, 1989. Norm, of course, was in the delivery room, along with my parents and Sherrie.

I made sure right away that Nichole did not have a cleft palate on her lip, which was a more common side effect from my medication. I was so relieved she did not, and I held her tightly to my chest. She was, for sure, our pride and joy, and we adored her. Later, as she grew older, her favorite animal was an elephant. I wonder how this came about, with her baby room decorated with elephant décor…haha!

Nichole, whom my brother Donald immediately nicknamed Niki, stayed home with me for an entire month after she was born. I was told not to expose my baby to anything outside the household for a month. After a month of being cooped up, we eventually went everywhere together! We headed to Tri-City Park often on foot, as I pushed her in the stroller in the mornings. Niki and I would travel around the lake at the park, with her enjoying the ducks and scenery, then we would head back home, as I was trying to lose some weight.

Norm and I brought her to church with us, but we did not leave her in the nursery. Not too long after she became a part of our now family of three, we decided to look around for a different church. After an approximately a year attending The Vineyard, we both found it hard to adjust to the charismatic doctrine, along with the practice of speaking in tongues, and I think this was our incentive to look around for something different.

We decided to try Rose Drive Friends Church, which was near our home. It had been there for many years, and I had often driven by and read a different Bible verse they posted each week on the corner sign. Nichole was about two or three months old, and we still brought her in the baby carrier to church service. We both loved listening to the pastor, C.W., preach. We decided that we were going to call this our new church, and we attended services there for almost twenty-seven years.

With Norm in the front as I sat behind him, Nichole became the third addition to our tandem. We continued taking little excursions on the bike, and Nichole often fell asleep as we rode. After about three months, we left Nichole over at her Grandma and Grandpa Palmer's to stay for a few days.

Norm and I went on our first trip away as new parents, to Carmel and Monterey Bay. It was our late anniversary trip, and we had a relaxing time alone. Each year following, we seemed to always take an excursion on or around our anniversary date.

In November, Sherrie and Pat had their second baby, a girl named Diana. She and Nichole were a little over five months apart. Our first Christmas was now going to be with a family of three, so we decided to put the Christmas tree on top of a corner table in the family room. Nichole began scooting backward, underneath the playpen next to the window, tables, our bed, and anywhere else her little body would fit. On Christmas, she was now able to sit up, and she did so among the wrapped gifts near the decorated tree.

Norm and I began attending a Sunday school class named The Seekers at Rose Drive Friends Church. We met many friends in Sunday school whom I still hold dear to my heart today. We learned more about the church through another class we took, and we soon became members.

There was a specific time, at the beginning of this class, that I was asked by a lady about my faith as a believer and if I had accepted Jesus in my heart. I responded abruptly, "Oh, why yes, I was raised Catholic all my life." Shortly after this occurred, I rededicated my life, thinking about this previous question I had been asked, through a special prayer offered by C.W., which he gave at the end of each Sunday sermon. Today, my life has grown stronger, deeper, and closer to my Savior, Jesus Christ, each day since that moment at RDFC.

*For great is your love toward me; you have delivered me from the depths, from the realm of the dead. But you, Lord, are a compassionate and gracious God, slow to anger, abounding in love and faithfulness* (Psalm 86:13, 15).

# ∽8∽

# Noticeable, Yet Untouchable

Nichole was soon to turn one year old in June. Boy, did we go all out for her first birthday celebration! We reserved a section at Tri-City Park and invited friends and family to join us on this big day. We even had a piñata to top off the party.

The following month, we took Niki and flew to Illinois to introduce her to my great-Aunt Marian and Uncle Franny. Sometime in July, I became pregnant again, and the new addition would arrive in April. I was tested again with an MRI to see if I was able to decrease or stop my seizure medication while being pregnant, but I was again unable to do so.

This same year, Norm had to go to the doctor to be checked, because he was bleeding at times while using the restroom. In 1990, at only twenty-eight years old, Norm had to have a colonoscopy to diagnose the problem further. They found polyps in his colon and said it was a genetic disorder called Gardener's Syndrome, or Familia Polyposis. The doctors told him to keep an eye on it and to have it checked every couple of years. We later found out that his grandfather died, although much older, on his mother's side, due to colon cancer.

During this second pregnancy, I gained about ten pounds more than I had gained with Niki. We could not decide on a name for a girl or boy that sounded good or that we both liked during these nine months of waiting. I found out from the ultrasound, before they decided to induce me the following day, that Norm and I were going to add a boy to our family! I kept this news to myself, though, so Norm would be surprised when I delivered. The Norton clan became a family of four on April 17, 1991. God blessed us with a healthy baby with no side effects from my seizure medication. Soon after the baby was born, we decided to name him Bryan Nelson, with the same middle name as Norm.

I began to be a very busy mom: taking care of two babies in diapers, cleaning and changing the bottle holders, feeding them, playing with them, picking up after them, cleaning the house, etc. We began potty-training Niki when she was around two years old, as we had been using cloth diapers to try to save money since I was a stay-at-home mom. Good ol' "Tidy-Dy-Dee Diaper Service" would come by our home once a week, taking the dirty and delivering the clean. It became a bit of a hassle, and so with Bryan, we began using disposable diapers instead, like most people did.

We did have a very small backyard/patio area at our condominium, which was between the sliding kitchen door and the door to the garage. Even though it was small, we had several playful toys in the tiny area, including a green turtle sandbox, a small children's red, yellow, and blue colored table, a large toy playhouse, and a red "sports" car.

I became involved in a Bible study once a week in the mornings at RDFC, as Niki and Bryan stayed with the other children in the nursery. The class was called Mothers and Others, and it was a time well spent learning more about the Bible.

I also became involved with a class called MOPS, which stood for Mothers of Preschoolers. This was where the moms would sit at tables in separate groups to get to know one another with a leader at each table. We would have small breakfast snacks and listen to a speaker. Afterward, we moms would answer questions given by the leader at each table, getting to know one another, and then doing art projects together.

I really enjoyed meeting new friends, becoming closer to friends I had previously met through the church, learning, and growing more in my faith. This was a particularly important time in my life, and I was so thankful that God sent me in this direction. I spoke in front of the smaller group of ladies in Mothers and Others one time, concerning the topic we were studying and relating it to my accident.

I spoke of what I had learned thus far during my recovery and in having a family of my own. I still had a future that I believed would continue growing closer to God in my process of healing. The following verse I used as the introduction to my speech:

*For you created my inmost being; you knit me together in my mother's womb. I praise you because I am fearfully and wonderfully made; your works are wonderful, I know that full well* (Psalm 139:13–14).

When Bryan was almost a year old, Norm and I spoke of buying a larger home. We were planning on having future children to add to the Norton family, as we had spoken before that we wanted to have six children. We were not seriously looking yet to move, but Norm would occasionally go look at homes for sale to check out the outside appearance and the neighborhood.

Norm soon came across a home, which we then drove by together so I could view it. Right away, before even seeing the inside, I said no! In this location, our kids in the future would have to attend Valencia High School and not my alma mater, El Dorado. Norm had said that by the time the children were old enough, we would move to a different location.

The same realtor who sold us our condominium showed us the inside of this house. We walked inside the home, and I totally did not like it! Most of the walls in the house were a dark brown color, and the carpet was an ugly brown. Also, I immediately said the kitchen island counter had to go.

Believe it or not, we bought this home, which had four small bedrooms and was almost 1,400 square feet in size! It had a pretty, spacious backyard, and Norm had said we would have the walls painted and install new carpet before we moved in. After we moved in, I slowly fell in love with the island counter in the center of the kitchen and I now use it daily, as I still live there today.

To add another minor detail in moving in, we moved three weeks before Niki's third birthday. Bryan had turned one the month before, and we moved at the end of May 1992. We hung pictures, quickly unpacked boxes, and set out all the knickknacks and decorations we could.

Of course, a birthday was going to be arriving soon, and we had to have another big birthday party with friends and family that included games, cake, and all the party essentials! We had the big celebration, and within a week after, Nichole and Bryan both broke out with chickenpox. I immediately had to phone all the parents to let them know ahead of time, in case their kids got it also.

We had our first Christmas in our new home, which I vaguely remember, but I do know that at one of our many Christmas celebrations, we began a habit of giving secret clues to finding gifts around the house. I do know that at this Christmas of 1992, I hid twelve different small gifts for Norm, going with the theme of the twelve days of Christmas. For the twelfth and last gift, Norm found a piece of paper hanging from the Christmas tree as an ornament. It had a surprise note telling him that I was pregnant with our third blessing; this addition to our family was due in September.

At this time, one of the spare bedrooms was a playroom for the kids, and both Nichole and Bryan each had their own bedroom. After the new baby was born, we then would decide who would share their room. We were all excited, especially Nichole, as she was our big girl, who really enjoyed helping and being the leader of the pack. Now she would enjoy another younger sibling and become more of Mom's little helper.

Nichole was the one in charge. She enjoyed dressing up as a teacher and playing school, with her siblings and friends as her students. She also enjoyed playing with Barbies and dressing up and putting on skits, magic shows, or talent shows—in front of an audience, of course.

Bryan, on the other hand, was more the one who loved building Legos, lining up trucks and cars, dressing up as either a fireman or a pirate, and playing as a little boy would, with dirt, bugs, and pretending to be at war with his friends outside. He was always busy thinking about what to do next. I think his mind often went faster than his feet!

Both children loved listening to Norm and I read them books, especially bedtime stories. They both would sit and listen, and I still remember their favorite books. Nichole loved *The Very Hungry Caterpilla*, and we read it so often, she soon memorized it and could read it back to us. Bryan was more interested in books about trucks and cars; one of his favorite books was *Are You My Mother?* It had an illustration of a "snort" truck on the page he enjoyed the most.

Nichole and Bryan were both late arrivals during pregnancy and had to be induced while Norm and I impatiently waited in the hospital. Well, the third arrival pretty much shocked us. We had been used to the regular routine of contractions, as we waited for them to be consecutive and closer together. On September 5, I was at home during the evening and began having contractions.

They were sporadic, and Norm stayed right by me to help me through each episode. The contractions began about thirty minutes apart, but they quickly changed to fifteen minutes, then jumped back to forty minutes, ten minutes, then thirty or something of that sort. You get the picture, the contraction times were changing quite often, but they stayed continuous. We waited and waited all night long, after phoning the doctor during the night. In the morning, St. Joseph's Hospital told us to come right in.

On September 6, 1993, Brittany Marie joined our family, just ten minutes after we arrived at the hospital! Brittany certainly had a lot of energy in my tummy those nine months, and this energy continued as she was growing up.

Her Aunt Sherrie gave her a little stuffed bunny when she was born, and she gave her niece the nickname, Brittany Bean. She carried that bunny everywhere as she grew up, and I still have it in her keepsakes, looking worn but loved. Again, Norm and I were relieved there were no side effects from my seizure medication, as I was tested before, but still unable to stop taking during pregnancy.

So now the Norton clan had four-year-old Nichole, who was given the nickname Small Fry as a baby by Norm; Bryan, who was now two and given the nickname Mr. Peabody, again by Norm; and Brittany Bean, nicknamed by Sherrie. Nichole and Bryan began to walk at around the age of one or a bit after, but Brittany decided to keep up with her brother and sister by walking at nine months old!

Brittany had light blond, curly hair, Bryan had straight, light blond hair, and Nichole had thick black hair. Brittany seemed to resemble baby photos of Grandma Palmer and myself. Brittany and I not only looked alike, but we had remarkably similar personalities. My actions, as I grew up, resembled a lot of my mom's attributes and actions, and it seemed Brittany followed the same path growing up. Bryan looked a little like Norm and a little like me. Nichole, on the other hand, resembled her dad quite a lot, both in looks and personality.

At age four, Nichole began a preschool class at Friends Christian School, two days a week. She could not wait to go, but it was sure hard for me to let go of my baby girl, even if it was just for a few hours a few days a week. Nichole was a strong-willed child with much confidence, and she showed this at an early age.

Brittany and Bryan became close and played well together. Brittany was a tomboy, but she loved to dress up in fancy dresses and high-heeled shoes, carrying around her bunny and joining Bryan as she climbed up on the pretend house out back in her dress-up attire. I had a box full of dress-up costumes and outfits, and they all enjoyed playing dress-up as they ran around the house and backyard.

Whenever I would take them shopping with me to a clothing store, Bryan and Brittany had the habit of playing hide-and-seek between the racks of clothes. Brittany did have a bit of a shy personality, but Bryan's eagerness to be active and talkative, like his dad, helped Brittany grow out of her shyness.

We had lots of toys and play equipment at our new home in the backyard for them. We had a large swing set, a bench swing, and a slide apparatus, and we added a monkey bar stand later as they got bigger. Norm also built a huge, two-story kid-size house, painted white, where they could play pirates, or whatever their imaginations came up with. As they grew, we managed to fit in a big trampoline that they and all the neighbors enjoyed continuously. All three of them kept me so busy, but I enjoyed spending the time with each of them growing up.

When Brittany was a walking toddler, we took our first motorhome trip to Newport Dunes. It was busy, yet relaxing on the beach, as our kids swam in the water and played in the sand. This was just the beginning of so many beautiful, memorable trips our family took together in the years ahead.

When fall came in 1994, school started for Nichole, who was now entering her first year of kindergarten! We decided to keep our children at Friends Christian School for as long as we could afford it. It was another big step for me as a mom to see my first child off on her own for about four hours, five days a week.

I cried as Norm and I led Nichole into her first day of school. She, of course, had a blast and could not wait to show me all that she had made at school and learned from her teacher. These were big steps our growing family took, with our oldest starting school and the beginning of Norm's medical condition that would be ongoing for many years ahead.

# ≈9≈

# Starting Anew

Norm went for his second or third colonoscopy to remove the polyps that the doctor had found. These would then be biopsied. It now had been about four years since he was first diagnosed with Gardeners Syndrome. After this procedure, the doctor informed us that he had found over one hundred precancerous polyps and told Norm he would need to have his colon removed to avoid developing colon cancer.

This was not easy news to absorb and process, especially since Norm was just thirty-two years old and a busy salesman, not to mention a father of three young children. Besides these busy roles, he was my best friend, husband, and lifetime faithful partner for eight years thus far.

My role as a wife became more important, and I needed to be a supportive, loving, compassionate, and confident partner in Norm's life. He had been this way for me in the past, during my slow recovery from the serious accident I had experienced. We cried together, we held each other closely, and we prayed together with friends, especially in our church and family. We then moved forward with the advice the doctor had given us.

Norm had his colon removed around the end of August 1994. He did pray quite earnestly with the doctor before the surgery began, and he asked if the doctor could do one more colonoscopy to make sure this procedure was needed. He felt that perhaps God had healed him, and the polyps would be gone. With me holding Norm's hand, the surgeon said that he was not going to check his colon again and then they took him in for surgery.

Norm woke up after his surgery and felt his abdomen right away. There was now a "J pouch" outside his stomach, which would remain there for three months. The pouch was to retain his stool and needed to be emptied by Norm quite often. He was in a lot of pain and certainly did not feel pleasant, changing this pouch and walking around with it on the inside of his shirt. After an extremely long three months of healing, he would undergo surgery to place the pouch inside of his body.

We did find out from his GI doctor that the genes from familia polyposis could be carried on to our children, and there was a 50 percent chance of them each having the same genes. We then decided we would have no more children and would be happy with the three blessings we now had in the Norton family.

Norm slowly got his energy back, and during that recovery, God brought yet another blessing to our family. After a month had passed since his surgery, we conceived, and I became pregnant with our fourth addition, due at the end of June. Our fourth and last child was certainly a gift from God that was not planned by us. Norm and I both needed to have our faith be strong and trust in the Lord that He would guide our paths along life's journey ahead.

*Trust in the Lord with all your heart and lean not on your own understanding; in all your ways submit to him, and he will make your paths straight* (Proverbs 3:5–6).

This had become my favorite verse from the Bible.

The gastroenterologist did say that Norm would have less energy, would take a while to heal, would be weaker, and might have occasional aches and pains from the absence of a major organ. He also would need to have an EGD to keep an eye on his stomach every year or so, to remove the polyps, and do biopsies to prevent them from turning to cancer.

Three months after his colon was removed, Norm had his follow up surgery, which brought another season of pain for him. This took some more time of rest and healing, but Norm was much more pleased without having the bag on the outside. It was placed inside and stitched back up, once more.

Time went on, and soon we would be having our next baby. My mom wanted it to be born, of course, on her birthday, which was June 29th. Well, sadly, her birthday passed with no baby, but on July 1, 1995, Sarah Suzanne joined our Norton family. She was born at St. Joseph's, and we were again happy another girl was added to our busy household.

We were young parents: Norm was 33, and I was 31; Nichole was six, Bryan was four, and Brittany was a few months shy of turning two. We were a close, growing family, and each child needed more and more energy from us parents, who were trying to raise them in a happy environment. We did it the best we knew how, at that time in our lives, and those were many of my favorite years to look back on.

Sarah had black hair when she was born, just as Nichole had. She was then, and is to this day, the duplicate of Nichole. With their looks as well as their personalities, both resemble their dad in many ways. Norm gave Sarah a nickname when she was born, "Pappachino." Yes, she was a bundle of happiness and a blessing. I was a lot stronger and wiser now as a mom, than I'd been when I had my first child, and when Sarah was approximately two weeks old, I brought her to church and dropped her off in the nursery.

In September, Bryan started four-year-old preschool class at Friends Christian School, two days a week. That was two less children at home for a few hours, at least two days each week. I would be able to spend more time with my little ones and try to catch up on my to-do list.

When Bryan was four years old, he was put in the hospital with pneumonia. He was there for several days. I stayed with him continuously, even during the night. It got so bad that one of his lungs collapsed, and he had a tube sticking out his left side. It was a difficult time for Norm and me, watching him go through this. Norm did bring in a few trucks and his white stuffed bear to hang on to.

Brittany and Sarah would often play with Barbies and Polly Pockets, play dress up and "house" with their baby dolls, or set up a grocery store. They would also have fun on the swing set, either in the backyard or at the park with me. During playtime they often would try to win the choice of what they would play with first.

Brittany loved to play with Barbie dolls, but Sarah would often choose Polly Pockets as her first choice. As you can probably guess, there were many disagreements on which one they would choose to play with first. Brittany would often try to make deals with Sarah just to get her way so they could play with Barbies first. Brittany would often win.

Sarah became a young star as a baby, playing a part in a large church Christmas musical. We were asked if she could play the part of the baby Jesus, while Norm would play Joseph and I would be Mary. Of course, we agreed to wear the costumes and enact such an important scene. It was a beautiful play; we were so proud to take part in it.

At a young age, Bryan began to spend a lot of his time writing little books on papers that I stapled together. He drew many detailed pictures to go along with the story he was writing. I still have many of those books in his keepsake box.

Sarah, on the other hand, would just like to collect any type of paper—whether it was trash paper, lined paper, plain paper, stickers, envelopes, you name it! If it was made of paper, she would collect it. I finally had to buy a large white box for her precious collection and tell her that if it didn't fit in the box, then she would have to get rid of another piece of paper or two to fit it in.

In June 1996, our family decided to go to Twin Lakes in Bridgeport. We rented a trailer to stay in. Norm rented a little boat to take out on the lake with Nichole, Bryan, and Brittany, as I stayed back at our campsite, taking care of Sarah. I think that was when Norm began falling in love with boats. We did have a nice time there, but it was quite cold, and there were many bears around, although they were mainly just interested in food found in the trash cans.

We decided to try it out again at Twin Lakes in August. We rented one of the same trailers as before, but this time Norm borrowed a boat from one of the owners of the company he worked at. He happened to be in the area at that time and let our family take the boat out on the lake. We all loved it and had a great time enjoying the outdoors. Sarah enjoyed it so much it put her to sleep, as I held her on my lap in the boat. We happened to be across the way of a family who rented a trailer and lived close to our home in Yorba Linda.

On that memorable trip, Norm had taken Nichole and Bryan out for a bike ride, as we often brought bikes with us on trips. I was just standing near the trailer keeping an eye on Brittany and Sarah, who were playing in the dirt and watching the deer, as we were surrounded by many tall, forest-green pine trees.

Suddenly, a branch broke off from one of those tall trees and dove quickly into my skull. It was stuck in my head, and I became scared due to my seizure disorder. The same family across from us offered to drive me to the emergency hospital about twenty or thirty minutes away, as Norm was still on the bike ride with the other two kids.

Norm arrived at the hospital shortly after I was admitted,

and the doctor mentioned to us that he had removed many, many fishhooks from patients in the past but never a tree branch! He had to shave off a little bit of hair for the procedure before stitching up the wound. This was a moment I will not ever forget, and thankfully I didn't have a seizure, but I did have a bad headache afterward.

In September 1996, Bryan was now old enough to be a "big boy" and start kindergarten. He was often reluctant to go to school, and when I would drop him off at his class, he would begin to really cry, which made me feel guilty leaving him. He did get a little better as time passed, but this lasted throughout the whole year, off and on. As I previously said, he enjoyed just hanging out back at home.

The following year was a busy year. Our family began using annual passes for Disneyland, which, back then, cost $99 per person. We bought the passes at Christmastime and enjoyed them for the following five years. Norm and Bryan often would get burned out waiting in long lines on many of the rides, though. Besides Disneyland, we brought our family of four enthusiastic children to places like Lego Land, Sea World, the San Diego Zoo, the San Diego Wild Animal Park, Knott's Berry Farm, and Magic Mountain. To add to that long list of amusement parks, we enjoyed places with water like the beach and Raging Waters, Wild Rivers, plus many other adventurous sights. We were a busy family.

During 1997, we decided to again rent a motorhome and take a trip to Big Sur and Pismo Beach. We took advantage of renting some individual water tubes for us to float on along the stream flowing by. We all took turns riding on them, and there was a certain incident that took place, which we recorded on video.

We were not keeping a close enough eye on our littlest one, Sarah. She was drifting down the stream, while I was close by on the shore with Nichole. I looked for Sarah, saw her drifting, and Nichole shouted that she would catch her. She ran and grabbed ahold of Sarah's tube before she floated on by. Luckily, Sarah did have on her floaties, but I was a bit worried there for a moment. Our last few days on the trip were spent at a motorhome campsite looking over Pismo Beach.

Another scene that stands out in my mind was in the motorhome, Nichole would lead Bryan, Brittany, and Sarah in singing various Christian songs, and on video, we recorded her leading her siblings in the song "Father Abraham." Too cute! Often, when we would get home from one vacation, Norm was busy online looking at ideas for our next vacation later that summer or the following year.

Beginning the school year, Brittany was now four years old, and she began attending preschool on Tuesdays and Thursdays at Friends Christian School. Now Brittany, being on the shy side, took some time getting to know people, but she was familiar with many of the faces from Sunday school. She enjoyed it, and this gave me one-on-one time to spend with our youngest, Sarah.

Around this time in our lives, we began to look further into how we could learn more about our children's health concerning the Gardeners Syndrome. Norm's mother later found out that she also had it, along with Norm's three sisters Fran, Mary, and Norma. We felt we needed to be proactive, since this gene seemed to be rapidly growing within the Norton family. Thus, Nichole and Bryan began having colonoscopies early in their lives to see if they had polyps in their colon. A few polyps were found in Nichole's colon, but nothing was found in Bryan's.

After each of them had had two procedures done, we had all four of our children tested genetically to see if they carried the genes. We felt we needed to know this information. After the testing was complete, we were told that two of our four children carried this disease, which was the 50 percent statistic we had been told at Norm's initial diagnosis.

The children who carried the gene were Nichole and Sarah, and so they would have to be tested every two years, including biopsies of any polyps removed from their colons. The same would be done for their stomachs if there were any polyps found there. Norm and I were determined to pray a lot and keep positive with this prognosis. We wanted to be "in front of the game" before it became serious and possibly turned to cancer for either daughter.

> *Do not be anxious about anything, but in every situation, by prayer and petition, with thanksgiving, present your requests to God. And the peace of God, which transcends all understanding, will guard your hearts and your minds in Christ Jesus* (Philippians 4:6–7).

I ensured that we had family photos taken each year before Christmas. We started this when the children were incredibly young, with planned outfits and different scenic areas. This seemed to always end up on the front of our yearly Christmas cards. My favorite family photo taken of the kids was when they posed next to a displayed reindeer and a huge ornament. Sarah was the one who made that photo so unique when she pressed together her lips for her smile and her arms were firmly bent with hands on her hips.

I believe this habit of mine began when I started becoming involved with friends at my church in making photo albums. It was so fun to look and reminisce at such cute photos of my growing family, and to decorate the scrapbook pages. I always seemed to be interested in keeping photos in albums as I grew up, but this became a hobby of mine when I was introduced to Creative Memories. This was the scrapbooking company who became well known in selling albums and all the needed décor for buyers to get hooked on putting together beautiful pages for memory and to show off to friends and family.

I think this was one of the interests I took from my mom, which was saving pictures and hanging them up for display. I previously had begun inexpensive, more condensed photo albums of Norm and I dating, adding to the ones of me as I was growing up. I also made collages from each of the many trips we took, which I will speak of throughout the following pages of the book. I still have many framed photos in the hall, kitchen, and bedroom that show the Norton clan's memories!

In May 1998, for our twelfth wedding anniversary, we again rode our tandem to Balboa, and after arriving, Norm had to fix a flat tire on our bike. After resting at our hotel, we ate dinner and walked along the pier. In the morning, we brought our breakfast up onto the upper deck and ate it as we overlooked the green-blue water below and the pale blue sky above.

We began our long trip heading home on the tandem, which usually took about four hours. Boy, our bottoms were sore when we arrived home! I believe after that trip, we decided to each purchase a bike of our own, as it was quite tiring for Norm to pedal and pull another person on the tandem, especially when we rode for long distances. On the bike trail, Norm would have to occasionally pull over to rest his right leg as it would often feel sore.

# ≈10≈

## Staying Busy, Yet Bound

Norm began looking around at boats for sale as he was interested in purchasing one for our family. We all went to a few places and checked out different boats, and Norm soon found a used one, which was only a year old. It did not have that much mileage on it, and so we decided to purchase it. The boat came with the ability to fish, which was one of Norm's favorite pastimes, along with water-skiing and cruising, which were a few of mine. This would add to our excitement for our future trips on the water for many years to come.

We first took the boat out to the ocean after Norm had it all fixed up and ready to go. He was quite excited, and the rest of us had smiles all over our faces. Our next adventure with the boat was to Lake Castaic, which was about one and a half hours away.

We had a fun time, but Norm was looking for even more of an adventure with our new toy in the water. Yes, we ended up heading to Lake Shasta in August 1998, and our family stayed on a houseboat. The scenery was beautiful, with tall green trees and blue sky, but the water was a bit chilly, at least for me. We all enjoyed the boat, along with going on short hikes and playing humorous family games at night.

We all were definite boat and water lovers, and if we were not at the lake in the summertime, our kids loved to go to the pools of either friends, the community, or their grandparents. Even water play in the front yard would do! We would set up a large pool filled with water and put their movable, small slide over it, so they could then slide down into the water.

We also had a slip 'n slide for them to have a blast with friends and many water toys to entertain the neighborhood with. Norm also would often join in and pretend to be a kid himself with water guns or getting into the kid's pool with them. Anything else they could come up with outdoors they did, using whatever pieces they found lying around.

When September rolled around, summertime was over. We had our first photo with all four children dressed up and ready to head off to school. This year, Sarah was beginning a three-year-old preschool class, meeting three times a week at Friends Christian School. Brittany now was enrolled in a Pre-K class. We made the choice to hold her back a year before she headed to kindergarten since she was on the young side and very petite. Bryan had moved up to second grade, and Nichole was in fourth grade. Wow, time had flown by!

Sarah was happy to join the group and be off to preschool, but it was not long before she began crying when I dropped her off. Norm and I soon chose to keep her home and thought maybe she was a bit on the young side, being only three years old. She was happy to again be home each day with Mom and run errands or play. After a month had passed, Sarah decided she was ready to try out preschool again.

When I took her there this time, she loved it! In fact, she became very involved in the class and showed more of the independent side of her personality. Not long after she was back, the teacher let Sarah be "in charge" of her classmates at times, as she would be preparing the next project for their day. Sarah would show them pictures in a book, sitting in front of her friends, or help the teacher in setting up craft projects or whatever was needed. She loved being the teacher's helper.

Since the kids were in school and I had a few days to myself for a couple of hours, I soon began a season where women of grade-school children would get together and pray for their kids.

This was called "Moms in Touch," and I genuinely enjoyed it and met several friends through the group. It was at the beginning of those many years I was involved with Moms in Touch, and lasted throughout Nichole, Bryan, Brittany, and Sarah's high school and college years.

Here I began writing down morning prayers for each of my precious children. I had written down each day of the week and listed different prayers for them, which became my daily routine in praying. I continue to pray for them, watching each grow with their individual characters. I often would read this prayer thinking of them, and I still do today, adding my three sons-in-law and my grandson to my prayer list:

> *I pray that out of his glorious riches he may strengthen you with power through his Spirit in your inner being, so that Christ may dwell in your hearts through faith. And I pray that you, being rooted and established in love, may have power, together with all the Lord's holy people, to grasp how wide and long and high and deep is the love of Christ, and to know this love that surpasses knowledge—that you may be filled to the measure of all the fullness of God* (Ephesians 3:16–19).

Now, back to my past experiences as a mother and the wife of a very special man. I was always trying to be in control, stay on task in organizing, playing with the kids, planning, cleaning, cooking, and whatever else might come up. From the beginning, I guess I began taking charge and giving instructions, being a bit selfish at times.

Nichole and Bryan had begun playing soccer on teams nearby, and Brittany and Sarah soon followed in their path. Sarah and Brittany first began through a group called Seahorse Soccer, which was a Christian organization they really enjoyed. They all also played throughout the years with JUSA and AYSO.

With Nichole, Bryan, and Sarah, it was usually every other year or so that they would join a team. With Brittany, though, soccer was her passion. She enjoyed it so much that it became a huge part of her life while growing up. She would continue playing each year, come rain or shine.

Around 1999 or 2000, Norm began getting frustrated easily, and he seemed to get more tired at times. He showed frustration at trying to teach Sarah how to ride a bicycle without training wheels. As a family, we took many bike-riding excursions. We would go hiking sometimes at Irvine Park and bring our bikes along with us. We often took our bikes to the trail off Jamboree, which went around and ended at Newport Dunes.

We did continue to stay interested in taking the boat out on vacations for many years from 1998 until 2013. For fifteen years, we took the boat each summer to one of these places: Lake Shasta, Lake Mohave, Lake Mead, Lake Havasu, Shaver Lake, Lake Powell, or Lake San Antonio, where we stayed in cabins or time shares, camped out, or stayed in a houseboat to add to the fun. Of those many years enjoying time with our boat, we rented houseboats for seven trips out of these fifteen exciting years. When it was just a trip for the day, we would head to Lake Castaic or Lake Pyramid.

I think Norm's favorite place was Lake Mead, where we went a few times and rented a houseboat. We took tubes so Norm could drive the boat and the kids would swing from side to side, do tricks like switching tubes while the boat was moving, or something crazy like that. Norm often made some sharp turns to watch them either hold on tight or fall off, and most of the time, he would laugh with them—if nobody was hurt from the wipeouts! We also had a set of wide skis, which I often used, and for the rest of the family, we purchased a knee board, a wake board, and all the other necessities for having a fun time in the water.

In 1999, we towed the boat and stayed in a houseboat for a week on Lake Mead. Joining us in the houseboat was another family. They had three kids close to Nichole, Bryan, and Brittany's ages, and the children enjoyed exploring together and having fun!

Soon after we bought the boat around this time, a friend at Southwest Controls, where Norm worked, was selling his jet ski, and asked if he would be interested in purchasing it. We all decided this would add to our excitement with the boat, so Norm bought it, and we brought that along on most of our following trips.

In 2000, we headed to Lake Shasta once again, hoping the weather would be a little warmer, as we were going a bit later in the summertime. One of the last nights there, a tremendous storm came, and the houseboats shook from side to side. It was quite scary and lasted through the night, so we decided to leave a day early.

As time went by, Norm would seem stressed out and anxious for much of the time during our "fun" vacations, and this kind of made me upset. I felt like we were supposed to relax and enjoy our family time away. He might have been thinking about the amount of money spent on trips away with our family. Or perhaps, he was having aches and pains from his previous surgery and ongoing disease, but he kept his feelings to himself.

Also, during 2000, Norm and I celebrated our fourteenth anniversary in July and traveled to Ireland. He had won a trip through his company for his great work as a salesman, and his two bosses at Southwest Controls paid for me to tag along and enjoy the country with him.

We enjoyed the short but exciting trip there, even though we got lost many times as Norm was steering a car. We were traveling quite a few roundabouts and often would end up heading in the wrong direction! We took many photos and were able to explore much scenery along the drive from the west coast of Ireland to the east coast. When Norm and I took trips alone, he seemed to enjoy them more and relax as we enjoyed one another's company.

In 2001, for our fifteenth anniversary, we rode bikes to Newport and stayed at Portofino Beach Hotel. Notice I mentioned "bikes," because a short time before, I had purchased a bike of my own. This made it a lot easier for Norm. After we woke up, we traveled home on our bikes—about twenty-five miles each way. We were exhausted, but we had a fun time together as usual.

After some time had passed since Norm's colon procedure, his mother, Cathy, was diagnosed with Familiar Polyposis and had to have her colon removed. There was cancer found in her colon, and in 2001, she passed away at sixty-five years old.

Within this timeframe, Norm's sister Norma also had her colon removed, as there were polyps present. As Norm did, she wanted to have her colon removed before cancer was found. When this took place, though, the hospital found that she had already cancer in her liver. They removed the cancerous portion of her liver, and she underwent radiation for some time after.

One of Norm's other sisters Fran had cancer in her colon along with many other health issues, too long to list. His sister Mary saw many different doctors and was trying to "cure" the cancer syndrome without having her colon removed. She was on medication, which she purchased from Mexico quite often. She also grew and ate grass, lettuce, and anything healthy and green. She had been told that this could keep the polyps from turning into cancer.

In July 2001, our family brought the boat with us and stayed in my parents' time share at Lake Havasu. Often, my parents would come and stay in Lake Havasu at the same time. Our family drove together to where the boat was stored and towed it out to the lake. Norm would often take control and try to do as much as he could on his own.

I am sure it took a lot of effort and work on his part, yet he did not want much help from the kids or me, even if we offered. Later, in August 2001, we rented another houseboat to spend a week at Lake Mead, where it wasn't as hot outdoors. Yes, the boat added many family times together, yet the close bonding I sought after seemed to be missing since we were so busy.

# ≈11≈

# Mountains to Climb

In 2002, another season in my life came along. Norm was having his EGD scope done again. He was told that he had multiple polyps in his stomach, some that might lead to cancer in the future. He was told he needed to have his stomach removed. First he had no colon, and now no stomach? How could he even survive? The doctor told us that it could be done, but Norm would be even more tired and weak, and when he needed to use the restroom, he would have little or no time to get there.

We were both shocked, upset, and heartbroken, and I remember going home, rocking in the chair, and praying to God that Norm and I would be taken care of in all circumstances. We knew it would be exceedingly difficult, but we scheduled an appointment a few weeks later with a surgeon.

*Be still, and know that I am God* (Psalm 46:10).

We went in to see the surgeon and asked many questions concerning the surgery that would take place. We had hoped the doctor would give us another solution, but he repeated the same information we had heard before. We left the appointment in tears. I tried my hardest to stay calm and to give Norm confidence in our decisions for his future. Norm was not one to procrastinate, so he went home and did a lot of research on Familia Polyposis.

After a bit of time passed, he came up with some information about how this disease was discovered. Norm was determined to dig deeper in finding out as much as he could in the short amount of time he had before the surgery was scheduled. He ended up hearing back from a research center in Utah called Huntsman Cancer Foundation in Salt Lake City. In between many phone calls, sending email information, and setting up a website regarding this gene, Norm scheduled a trip to Utah soon after.

Norm and I set up plans for where our kids would stay for the few days we would be gone. He was again scheduled to have an EGD scope done for a clinical trial at the University of Utah. We were told that they would make hotel accommodations for both of us to stay on the same campus as the research hospital. You see, the doctor who had discovered this gene was from Utah, and his name was Dr. Gardener.

Ultimately, the doctor in Utah told Norm afterward that no, he did not need to have his stomach removed! It would be highly unlikely for the stomach polyps to turn into cancer, as the gene had only been found to cause this to happen two percent of the time in people with this syndrome. Hallelujah! Because of Norm's research and perseverance, we now saw a cure for the sad news we had previously heard. His determination paid off when the doctor let him know such great news. We were both so thankful, and we praised the Lord for watching over us in good times and in bad.

> *You've always been great toward me—what love! You snatched me from the brink of disaster! ... You, Lord, are a compassionate and gracious God, slow to anger, abounding in love and faithfulness* (Psalm 86:13,15 MSG).

Life went on at the Norton household, and Nichole became a cheerleader when she was in sixth grade with a Pop Warner football team. She seemed to enjoy it, so she continued as she headed on to middle school. Bryan was playing flag football, along with soccer and Upward Basketball through our church. He was extremely competitive and determined, just like his dad was. Norm was his coach a few times in soccer and with Upward Basketball.

Brittany continued her love for soccer. She occasionally joined a team in Upward Basketball, along with Sarah. While our kids were involved in Upward Basketball, Norm presented a devotion several times at halftime. This was a usual tradition, listening to different devotions given by adults at halftime. Norm's devotions were all centered on the same theme of teaching us to be "Fishers of Men." He also taught on this same topic in adult Sunday school classes.

You do remember how I mentioned earlier that Sarah loved to collect paper. She became really interested in taking an art class once a week at an incredibly young age. We signed her up at Kids Art, and so her true interest began for the love of painting, drawing, and charcoal.

Around this time, Norm was asked by a different company called Mag-trol Long Beach, Inc. to come and work for them. Now he was faced with another big decision concerning changing his employment from the company that he had been with for many years. Norm wanted me to meet the owner of the company along with his wife and children. He wanted to get a closer view of his personality with work, as well as at home.

Our family was invited to their home in Malibu, and Bryan and Sarah were the two who joined Norm and me to meet with them. We had dinner with them, and afterward, Bryan took advantage of going for a ride in the owner's Porsche. When we left, Norm and I talked and prayed about it that evening. He then accepted this new position at Mag-trol Long Beach as an outside salesman, mostly doing business at the ports in Long Beach.

When our three girls were young, we had them also involved in ballet, theater, and acting. They went to weekly practices and did yearly performances onstage. In one of the plays, Nichole was Dorothy in *The Wizard of Oz* while Brittany and Sarah played the part of the munchkins. They did such a cute job playing their parts for the large audience and being stars onstage. As they got older, though, Nichole wanted to begin taking cheer classes, while Brittany and Sarah became interested in gymnastics.

Bryan, at the time, was busy playing with neighborhood or school friends out in the backyard or in front practicing soccer or street hockey, where he often played as the goalie. If not outside, he might have been studying for an upcoming spelling bee, in which he often did quite well, reading history books, or collecting coins from a place in Yorba Linda.

Bryan always kept his mind busy. As he was growing up, he and I seemed to have a bond. We communicated with each other well. Bryan would, at times, come to me when he needed his mom's advice or a shoulder to cry on. It became a habit, since he was a very little boy, for me to sing to him after we said prayers together at night. Other times Norm would go in and tell Bryan a story he would make up, which was often funny, before he would close his eyes for the night.

During the time our kids were growing up, we also began sending them to summer camps called Quaker Meadows through Rose Drive Friends Church. This camp was for a week, and they enjoyed being independent. There were a few times I volunteered as a counselor at these camps, for both Brittany's group of peers and Nichole with her set of friends, at different times.

Once, when Bryan went to Quaker Meadow, I believe when he was going to be entering sixth grade, and I helped him pack his suitcase before he left. A week later, when he arrived back on the bus, he was wearing the same clothes he had left home in!

I made him take off his clothes in the garage, and there was a line of dirt from where his socks had been glued onto him for the week. He had never taken a shower or changed his clothes! I did find out that on the first night away, Mr. Homebody, Bryan, cried himself to sleep, as he was so homesick. In the morning, he awoke like nothing had happened, and he had a fun but dirty week away.

Nichole was a cheerleader for Friends Christian School during her seventh and eighth grade years, which were 2001 through 2003. She thoroughly enjoyed it, and so did Norm and I during the many times we watched her perform. I went to all her games; basketball and football, and Norm went to the ones he could fit into his busy work schedule.

Toward the end of her eighth-grade year, a friend of ours from church mentioned something to us about Nichole's posture and hip. This lady had a daughter who had recently had to have surgery for a crooked spine, and she suggested maybe we should have Nichole's spine checked out. We followed through and had X-rays taken.

Her spine was crooked, and we followed the doctor's advice, which was for her to try to keep good posture and be fitted for a brace to wear at night. We would then follow up with the doctor in a year. She continued cheering on the squad, performing her talented front flips, up in the air, but as time went on, the issues with her spine continued to get worse.

Around this time in our lives, another health issue occurred, and this time it was with me. It seemed the more I drove to various places, the more my right leg began hurting, especially when I was driving in traffic. With four kids all involved in different activities or even taking them to and from the beach, I drove a lot. The soreness in my leg was due, again, from the accident.

A dear friend told me about a chiropractor who might be able to help. I still see the same chiropractor today, and the pain has been healed.

During this period in our family's life, though, we faced various obstacles that God led us through by others who were put in our paths.

# ⁓12⁓

## Watched As a Hawk

In August 2003, we traveled to Lake Mohave. While on our houseboat, the Medina and Mohr families came to visit for a day and took some rides on the boat, and we all had a blast! I remember Debbie and I resting on some boogie boards out in the lake with our chips and salsa and sodas, drifting around with the snacks on top of the boards. It was very relaxing, along with our oh-so-slow cruises on the tubes as Norm drove the boat.

While Bryan was in middle school at FCS during his sixth and seventh grade, he wanted to volunteer our home to a Korean student whom the private school was sponsoring. We agreed with Bryan and thought it might be a fun experience. During his sixth-grade year, a boy named Owen came to stay with us for six weeks. We loved him!

Owen and Bryan went to school together; we took him to church with us; and we brought him on many scenic outings, including to the beach, tide pools, Dana Point, Magic Mountain, and to Koreatown in LA. He spoke English well enough for us to understand him, and he wanted to continually learn more while in America. Bryan and Owen became remarkably close to one another, and Owen seemed to learn more about his Christian faith. It was difficult saying good-bye to Owen when he flew back to Korea.

In May 2004, we decided to make some improvements to our home. As the kids were all growing up, we had thought about adding on and enclosing the back patio so that we could add a recreation/TV room. It would be more spacious for our growing family. Nichole then convinced us, "No, we can just fix it up inside, because it is large enough for all of us to live in, just the size it is!" So, we took her advice and began having a lot of changes done inside to make it look more up-to-date.

Of course, we would always bring our dogs along for the trips on the houseboat or camping. In August 2004, we brought our two dogs, Shasta and Holly, with us to stay on the houseboat at Lake Mohave. (By the way, Shasta was Norm's favorite of all the dogs we owned.)

Neighbors of ours came to visit us for the day, and we were relaxing in chairs, on shore, while the kids were playing in the water and the dogs were wandering around near us—or so we thought. Suddenly, we heard the loud bell ringing from another houseboat parked not too far away, and Norm thought, *Where are our dogs?*

He ran over to another houseboat, wandering through the bushes. It just so happened that Shasta had gone onto this stranger's houseboat and begun barking, as our dog thought the couple on board were strangers on our boat. Norm apologized and brought her and Holly back to our area, and we kept a closer eye on the dogs from then on.

When Nichole began high school at Valencia, she was on the varsity cheer squad for her freshman and sophomore years. We were again traveling to games to watch the squad cheer, see the many games, and go to competitions. I would have my van full of cheerleaders traveling to an event and to car washes to raise money. Norm and I were continually going to soccer games, as well, when in season, to watch Brittany, along with Sarah and Bryan when those two felt like joining a team.

Bryan began to enjoy playing chess during his recess while his other friends were playing soccer or basketball. Something we began noticing with Bryan at home was that his grades began going down toward the end of his seventh-grade year. In his math class, he would just put the answer down without going through the whole process of figuring it out and showing his work. He already knew the answer!

Norm and I were concerned, and after speaking to him more about it, we discovered Bryan was bored in his classes. We were advised to have him tested through FCS. The results showed that he needed to be in a more competitive academic atmosphere, such as the "Gate" program. Bryan's grades had been going down because of his unfinished work. His schoolwork was not challenging enough to keep his interest.

We chose to send him to Kraemer Middle School in his eighth-grade year, where he was able to learn through a "Gate" program. In doing so, we also found out that Bryan had to be placed in a lower math class, and that the private school was behind, at that time, in various subjects when compared to the public school.

In seeing this, we began to think of Brittany and Sarah and their years ahead. Brittany and Sarah did not mind making the switch, and after interviewing with the principal at Van Buren Elementary School, we made the choice to switch all three of them to public school in 2004 for the next school year.

I would volunteer weekly in my younger girls' classrooms to help the teachers out and see my favorite students in the class. I also began to work for their school and help as the lunch lady. I took on this role as Sarah began her elementary years, both at Friends Christian School, and then I continued after being hired on through the Placentia Yorba Linda School District, working at Van Buren Elementary School.

A side note: I did begin to make it a habit when they were in high school to take them personally out to lunch once a week when they had their lunch break and free time to leave campus. As a mom, I really enjoyed this one-on-one time with them each week.

During this same year, in 2005, Mary, Norm's sister, had her colon removed because the doctor had found cancer. After the surgery was over, Norm, Mary's daughter Audry, and I went downstairs to the lab and were shown the actual colon that had been removed. It was shown to us in a large, clear container by the surgeon in the hospital. It was very weird to actually see a part of her body, a part that was sadly bringing about so many problems within the Norton family. We were also shown all the polyps that had been causing these prolonged issues.

Nichole was finishing up her second year as a varsity cheerleader that year. I planned a surprise party for her sixteenth birthday in June. The celebration was at our home, and sneaky Niki found out about it the day before the party. I had invited her friends from church and friends from her cheerleading squad to join us for her sweet sixteen birthday bash.

Nichole also began a job when she was almost sixteen. She became a hostess first, then a waitress at an Italian restaurant called Paolinis. Also, at the end of her sophomore year, Nichole began to like a guy named Frank. They had met each other in Sunday school at RDFC, and after she turned sixteen, we allowed her to go out on a date with Frank.

Before Bryan began high school, he took lessons playing the electric and bass guitar. When he was younger, he had previously taken piano lessons, and he could play the electric organ we had at home. As he learned more with the guitar lessons, he and a few neighborhood kids put together a band called Down Jefferson. All the boys in the band, at one time, lived off our main street, which was called Jefferson. They would perform in various places, such as downtown Fullerton, as a side band, at a night club with other bands, and we would go and listen to them play.

Also, at the same time, in between singing lessons and some piano lessons, Brittany continued playing soccer. She was not interested in getting tested and involved in the "Gate" program in school. Brittany was happy and content with classes that would not take too much of her time and effort, as she would rather be on the field kicking the ball or running. Norm and I both loved watching her determination in running races and playing soccer!

Sarah began in the "Gate" program throughout her years in middle school. She was busy spending her free time in her art class and beginning to take it a few times during the week. As she got a bit older, we took a walk together as a family in Laguna and looked at all the beautiful art galleries.

Sarah began becoming even more interested in her art talents after speaking to an artist at her gallery in Laguna. This precious elderly lady became one of Sarah's most meaningful mentors along the journey. Later, in the years to come, this artist displayed one of Sarah's fine pieces of art in the front window of her popular gallery.

Then came the time when we had to decide on another important health issue. Nichole's spine was again checked, and the doctor told us that she was done growing in height. Her spine had gotten worse. When her yearly X-rays were taken, her spine now was almost in a perfect S shape.

Close friends from church had introduced us to a couple whose son had experienced the same issue. They gave Norm and me a surgeon's name located at Cedar Sinai Hospital. After seeing the doctor, we made an appointment for Nichole to have surgery to put a rod in her back. The surgery was going to take place during the summer of 2005, before her junior year of high school.

We decided as a family to go on a boat trip at the beginning of July 2005, before her surgery took place. We were going to Lake Havasu and stay in one of Mom and Dad's time shares. Frank went along, as well, and brought his jet ski. On this trip, Frank and Nichole were not spending much free time with

Norm and me, which was making me incredibly sad and a bit jealous of all the time Nichole shared with Frank, away from our family time.

I also have memories of hearing about a four-day camping trip during the summer that Norm went on with Bryan, which was offered to students in their high school years through the church. This camp was at Lake Nacimiento and was referred to as "Lakefest." Of course, Norm would bring his boat along for entertainment, pulling inner tubes, swinging his boat from side to side, and doing donuts, which he loved most of all.

The time came in our lives where we began to grow distant from Nichole, as it was exceedingly difficult to face our little girl growing up, her having a boyfriend, and us letting her go. She had been wanting her independence, and Norm and I were still watching over her and not letting her grow up. Her surgery and recovery went remarkably well, but it was during this episode that I began to grow further apart from her and saw Frank and Nichole draw closer together.

As a side note, not too long ago, Nichole reminded me that after her surgery, I had watched over her like a hawk, not even letting her watch too much television during her recovery. Of course, the classes that Norm and I attended in the past had taught us as parents not to let our kids watch too much TV or even hold hands with a boyfriend, "as one thing could often lead to another." Sorry to say, but Nichole was like our practice round in raising children. Our actions, though, sad to say, caused her to spend more time in her last years of high school with Frank and his family.

# ⟊13⟋

# Time to Leave

On May 31, 2006, Norm and I were planning on celebrating our twentieth anniversary. Nichole took the initiative, along with the other kids, to plan a surprise weekend for us. Norm and I had no idea that something was being planned behind our backs. We received little typed-up notes preparing us for what each surprise would entail. We first went to dinner, and then they had booked us a night at the Homestead Studio Suites.

The next morning, a note in our suitcase told us to leave by 9:15 and head to Newport Beach Back Bay Café, where we were to have our brunch. We then read our next hint from a note, which stated that we were to be home no earlier or later than 1:00 p.m. sharp. We arrived home, and our kids (with probably a few helpers) had planned a beautiful anniversary party with dear friends and family.

To this day, my heart warms at how special of a time that was! After a lovely day celebrating with food and cake, there was the next surprise typed on another note, saying that Andy and Lisa had reserved a night at The Tides Inn in Laguna. We were off again to the beach. We brought along our bikes and had a wonderful time spending time together in Laguna, where we had begun our engagement twenty years before. We ate breakfast at Greeter's Corner, where we had gone the first morning on our honeymoon.

As a mom, I certainly was not looking forward to the day when Brittany and Sarah asked me if I would stop working at their schools as a lunch lady or in their classrooms. Brittany was at Kraemer Middle School in seventh grade, and Sarah was about to begin fifth grade. I had extra free time because of this, so I felt it was time for me to begin a real job, and I applied with the school district to work with special needs students.

I had to first take an exam covering materials such as math and English, as I did not have an AA degree. I took a class offered for a review of math and when I took the exam covering both, I passed it with a 94 percent and was so proud of myself. I was hired on at George Key School, this time through the district, and I began working with students aging from thirteen to sixteen. Maybe I could have made it if I chose to go back to college, but my life was busy now with a family.

The following year, in April 2007, Bryan turned sixteen, and both Norm and I planned a surprise birthday party for him. Since he was so into music, singing and playing his guitar in his band, Down Jefferson, we invited friends and family, and we hired a band made up of guys whom he knew, who played in our backyard during the party. He was very surprised, and it was a loud, fun celebration.

During Nichole's senior year of high school, she began taking classes at Fullerton Junior College on the side. While doing so, she quickly decided how much she enjoyed her accounting class, in which she was enrolled there, so she changed her major from cosmetology to accounting. Nichole was only taking her last four classes required for her to graduate high school, so she had the time and took advantage of it.

Nichole graduated from Valencia High School in 2007. She was far beyond ready to make her next step in life, and that was to begin college. We did have an open house graduation party at our home for us all to celebrate her accomplishments. At her party, I had displayed her photo albums, which showed her past four years of high school memories.

Although we tried to talk her out of it, Nichole was determined to move to Arizona and attend Northern Arizona University. Her boyfriend, Frank, had moved to Arizona two years before to attend college at Embry Riddle Aeronautical University. Also, Nichole had said the school offered great opportunities for an accounting degree. She was very independent, and she wanted to live on her own and begin her future as an adult.

Norm told her that we could only afford to pay for a state school, and we would not be able to help her pay for room and board. It was difficult letting our firstborn go to such a distant place, but we knew in the back of our minds that she was growing up, becoming more independent, and we tried our hardest to let her do so.

During the summer of 2007, our family took a camping vacation. Yes, I was going to try to camp out. Norm had several times been camping in the past before we met. I had never camped like this before, but I thought I would give it a try. We headed to Lake San Antonio.

Nichole had left before us with Frank's family, and she chose not to join us on our first family camping excursion. Instead, she slept with Frank's family in their motorhome and spent most of her time with the Petersons. We took the boat and jet-ski and had a lot of fun in the water. We also played a full game of Monopoly under a canopy tent, next to our sleeping tents, closely lined up.

The following month, we decided to meet Frank's family and Nichole at Lake Powell with our boat, but we chose to stay in a place inland, as camping really was not my thing. This was going to be our last trip with Nichole before she was off to Arizona for college.

Nichole stayed again with Frank's family in their motorhome. We also took a scenic tour of Prescott, where Frank showed us his college nearby. It was difficult for me to watch my daughter Nichole becoming so much a part of Frank's world now, and I certainly was jealous and sad to see another piece of her heart growing further apart from us.

Bryan began his first job at the age of sixteen, working at Lakeview Café, but he did not get his driver's license until he was almost seventeen years old, during his junior year. He was a waiter, and we often went there for breakfast or lunch to visit and give him a good tip as he waited on our table.

Brittany played her last year with the club soccer team she grew up with, the "Breakers," that had become a huge part of her life and ours. The team stayed together for about six to seven years, as they kept playing weekly games, often winning in various tournaments. We parents kept cheering them on wherever we would travel.

Yes, we did much traveling, and as Bryan and Sarah got older, they lost interest in going with Norm and me to cheer Brittany on. When we would go away for a weekend, Sarah would often choose to stay at a friend's house or with Grandma and Grandpa Palmer. Bryan would be busy with his new job and his friends, so he would stay behind too, whether it was for a day or a few days. Norm and I would be Brittany's good ol' soccer clan.

Sarah played as a goalie in soccer most of the time, the same as Nichole and Bryan. When Sarah was not playing soccer or inviting a friend to come over to hang out, she was busy painting. Hanging in our family home are many of the beautiful paintings she has created, and so I display them and show them off. As our kids got older and adventured ahead, I needed to try the difficult independence of being a mom.

# ⟨14⟩

# Tears to My Eyes

Yes, now began the next season in my life with my family. Bryan, Brittany, and Sarah were all growing up so fast. Bryan was now a junior at Valencia, he was done playing soccer either at school or on other teams. He just played it for fun, but he loved to mostly watch it on TV. In fact, to this day, he watches professional teams play on television. Brittany was entering her last year at Kraemer Middle School, and Sarah was ending her last year at Van Buren Elementary.

Nichole was beginning NAU in 2007. We traveled to Arizona with our truck packed with Nichole's belongings. Frank and his family came to help move Nichole into her dorm room. It was a huge transition for me to accept that my first daughter was off to college, so many miles away. Deep down, I knew the time had come that I needed to let go and continue praying that God would direct her and keep her safe.

*And this is my prayer: that your love may abound more and more in knowledge and depth of insight, so that you may be able to discern what is best and may be pure and blameless for the day of Christ* (Philippians 1:9–10).

Toward the end of September 2007, and at the beginning of Nichole's first year at NAU, Sarah and I took a train to visit her for "family weekend." We spent the night on the train both to and from Fullerton to Flagstaff. We had a pretty nice time visiting Nichole. We were able to tour the campus and see where her classes would take place.

85

Before Christmas in past years, our family had bought gifts for children who did not have a family to celebrate Christmas with or the money to buy gifts. We would have the kids pick a name off a Christmas tree in the back of the church with a boy or girl close to their age. Norm and I would try to teach our children the importance of giving.

We also began to help a family whose name we received through a nonprofit business called Canning Hunger. During Thanksgiving time each year, we would also purchase a "Box of Love" through Canning Hunger, to fill with a holiday meal with all the trimmings for a family to cook and eat for the holidays.

One year, we had met a family who lived close by and went over to their apartment to bring them a Christmas tree, gifts, and a "Box of Love." In talking with the family with our kids by our side, we all prayed in a circle for their needs and for their health. After the prayer ended, I was led to invite them to our home on the afternoon of Christmas Eve, to join us for dinner. They were so happy and said they would bring tamales, and boy, did they ever! This meant so much to me personally, and I began to grow in this routine of giving, thanks to Norm's inspiration.

> *In everything I did, I showed you that by this kind of hard work we must help the weak, remembering the words the Lord Jesus himself said: "It is more blessed to give than to receive"* (Acts 20:35).

We also began a tradition at Easter. As our kids were younger, Norm had built a wooden cross for the kitchen table as a centerpiece. We each wrote a note with something we were thankful for and a specific prayer request, placing it near the cross that was always our centerpiece during Easter. On Easter, we would read each slip of paper and pray for one another.

Summertime was upon us in 2008, and we planned another trip camping and towing our boat. We headed again to Lake San

Antonio and stayed in the same area as we had previously. Frank's family and some of their friends, along with Nichole, also traveled there in their motorhomes. Of course, I was a jealous mom who wanted more of Niki's attention. We spent some time over at Frank's family circle of chairs, sharing dinner with them and talking.

Most of the time, though, our family hung out at our camping site, on our boat, with our tubes, boat toys, and jet ski. Norm and I did not really converse with them a lot, as we felt a bit uncomfortable in their surroundings, as Nichole was continuing to gather her independence. This was the last trip we took with Frank and Nichole at the same time. We did not see Nichole around our house much either while she was home from college for the summer.

The school year started again, and Nichole was off to her second year at NAU. Bryan was a senior in high school at Valencia, and Brittany had just begun her high school year as a freshman. Sarah was moving on to Kraemer Middle School in seventh grade. A new year had begun all over again with our rapidly growing kids.

I will begin with one of the most meaningful times for Bryan's career plans in the future. He met a boy at school about a month after the school year began and came home one day asking us a question I will never forget.

He asked, "Mom, Dad, could we have a foreign exchange student come stay with us?"

We answered, "Sure, for how long?"

Bryan replied, "For the whole school year."

Norm said, "We will pray about it and let you know."

Norm and I prayed together. After speaking to the company in charge to find out more details and information before we made this large decision, we let Bryan know that his friend would be welcome in our home. They could share a room, and the bunk beds, which were in Brittany and Sarah's room at the time, would be moved into his room.

The foreign exchange student's name was Anton, and he was from Germany. He had made previous plans to stay with a couple who now were in the process of a divorce, so Anton had been put in a temporary home with a busy, working lady who had no other children for him to hang out with. He had met Bryan at school, and they got along very well. Bryan thought our family would be a great fit for Anton.

When high school began, Brittany was on the varsity team as a freshman, and Barry, a close friend of ours, was her coach. Many years before, my kids had all been a part of Barry and Krysten's wedding, as Krysten had babysat our children when they were very young, each Tuesday night. Norm and I would head out to eat and then go to our weekly Bible study. We had known Krysten through her parents with whom we shared a lot of time in Sunday school for many years.

Brittany also took a big liking to cross-country running while at Valencia. Norm and I would watch her and the Valencia team at different meets, usually held at large parks. For several years, Brittany was also on another club soccer team called the Fullerton Rangers. Norm and I both kept traveling and watching her play on weekends, wherever they might be heading.

There were many occasions when my mom and I would travel alone with Brittany to the games, and Norm would stay at home. We would watch Brittany play soccer at such places as San Francisco, Santa Maria, or Las Vegas, and stay at a hotel with the team. My mom and I had such an enjoyable time traveling together; we would laugh so hard that tears would run down our faces!

Norm and I didn't yet leave Sarah home alone, as she was still too young. When we would both go to the games, Sarah would either join us or quite often, she chose to stay with a friend. I had asked Bryan and Sarah if they were bothered by Dad and Mom leaving for the weekend or an entire day to watch Brittany play, while they were left behind. Both said they were not bothered with it.

# ⪜15⪛

# Two Shall Become One

In 2008, after two years working at George Key School, I decided to advance my career and begin working with autistic students. I was interviewed again at the district office, hired, and began my training at Mabel Paine Elementary School.

I had training for almost two months, working one-on-one with preschool students and learning how to use the DTT—District Trial Training process. I was taught how to mark down their progress with data while trying to keep my energetic student content. I was so happy and proud of myself that I could get this far, considering the effects on my brain from the accident, and enjoy the work I was able to do.

The second year, I worked with a teacher who helped me learn so much more on working with autistic students. I read a large book he recommended, titled *A Work in Progress*. I have now worked twelve years in this field, dedicating my patience and efforts to students with autism.

The class I work in now is known as "the clinic" at Tyne's Elementary School. The clinic has the most severe autistic students who begin school at age three. I love my job and am thankful that I have the ability, interest, and patience to call this my career.

*I can do all this through him who gives me strength* (Philippians 4:13).

Anton was a huge part of our family for that school year, and he still is today. At the beginning of the school year, once he felt comfortable with our family, he made himself well known in the bleachers at the Friday night Valencia football games. As we sat in the stands watching the players on the field, Anton would act as a cheerleader in the bleachers.

He would turn to face all the people watching the game, raise up his arms, and tell the fans to join him in shouting, "Go, Valencia Tigers, go!" A bit later in the year, he would also go to Brittany's soccer games at Valencia and cheer them on, shouting, "Go, Lady Tigers," or "Go, Brittany!"

That year we had an enjoyable Christmas celebration with our family along with Anton. I did make him a personal Creative Memories album with photos in it, along with many more to add to it in the following months ahead. We also bought him a Bible that he could take home with him.

We did see his parents and Anton's brother when he would Skype them, but we did not understand what they were saying. Bryan began to take an interest in the German language. Anton had a book with one page in English and the other in German, both saying the same words.

During their high school years, our kids were all involved in mission trips to Mexicali during Easter break at Rose Drive Friends Church. Yes, the students were willing to give up their vacation time from school to minister to others in need. The groups were set up to go to minister at different villages with such tasks as hanging around with the kids, joining them with arts and crafts, or playing soccer. They were humbly teaching the villages more about their strong Christian beliefs with their presence, love, and actions.

They would camp out there, and they seemed to grow closer to God themselves on this trip, with the purpose to communicate and teach less fortunate people about Jesus. Bryan did not attend the Mexicali trip during his senior year because Anton could not leave the United States. I do not think Bryan was too interested in going anyway. He began to be less interested in attending church, yet he and Anton would attend each week with the family.

On May 17, 2009, Frank and Nichole were married after dating for four years. The wedding took place about two weeks after Frank graduated from college. Nichole still had just one more semester left. I had tried to convince them to wait until at least after Nichole's birthday in two weeks, when she would turn twenty. I thought that would sound so much better to tell their future kids that she was not just nineteen at the time, but twenty years old when they were married. They said no, and their wedding plans proceeded.

When the special day arrived, Bryan, Brittany, and Sarah were all part of the wedding party. Anton took part in escorting Bryan's girlfriend in the wedding, which was in Dana Point on a hill overlooking the ocean. Norm and I both did not feel very involved in the planning of their wedding or taking part in helping Nichole and Frank with the details that usually the mother of the bride handles.

The reception was located at Laguna Community Center. I remember crying during the wedding, happy yet sad, as my first and oldest daughter was now getting married and permanently moving out for good! I also cried at the reception at our table as I sat next to Norm, who was holding me close to him. I felt a big loss inside my heart as I felt Nichole and I growing even further apart.

In June 2009, Bryan graduated from high school. Our second child was growing up and starting on a new direction in his life! Soon after, the time came when Anton had to return to Germany. It was extremely hard saying good-bye. Our family had grown so close to Anton, and we were looking forward to someday visiting Germany and meeting his family. This time, however, Bryan chose to fly back to Germany for the summer and meet Anton's family.

At the end of the summer, Bryan returned home from Germany and began a new job. He chose not to go with Norm, Brittany, Sarah, and me on our summer vacation. Bryan had been hired at Macaroni Grill, and since he had not been working and making an income during the summer in Germany, he decided to stay at home.

We all spent a week in San Juan Capistrano at my parents' time share, which was across the street from the beach. We went on a cruise to Catalina for the day and adventured on a self-guided tour driving a small cart to view Catalina from the top, looking down from the hillside toward the ocean below.

Toward the end of our vacation week, we celebrated Brittany's sweet sixteen September birthday. Sad to say, though, it was not a very enjoyable trip as Norm hadn't been feeling too well, with a cough and cold starting before our trip began. Then, his expensive bike was stolen right outside our family room on the patio, as we were sitting next to the sliding door, watching a movie, earlier in the week. We heard something outside, but we had thought it might be the wind or traffic because we were next to the main boulevard.

In September, Bryan began his first year of college at Cal State Fullerton, Brittany was now a sophomore at Valencia, and Sarah was finishing her last year in junior high at Kraemer. Around this time, Bryan began to drift further away from his faith and closeness with God. He no longer wanted to go with us to church, but we firmly told him that while he was living in our home, he needed to go to church. If he was not growing in his faith or felt like he did not fit in at Rose Drive Friends Church, we suggested maybe he could find another church to attend.

After we suggested this, he chose a Unitarian church he located online. Norm and I joined him on one of the first Sundays he began attending. After hearing the service and finding out through reading more about their beliefs behind this "religion," we were stunned! The church taught that everyone would go to heaven if they were good people.

After that experience, we stepped back as overbearing parents and told him he did not need to go every week to church. He had chosen this church with beliefs that were the extreme opposite from our Christian faith that we had raised him in. He might have done this in defense of us or with a genuine interest; who knows? Bryan then decided that he was no longer going to attend church.

That Thanksgiving, Brittany, Sarah, and I went on a train trip to visit Nichole and Frank in Flagstaff. Nichole was finishing up her last semester of school, and we had made plans beforehand to go visit and have a "girls" trip. We ate an early afternoon Thanksgiving meal on Thursday with Frank, and then the four of us gals headed to Las Vegas, Nevada!

We had our gift ideas and were ready to go midnight shopping on the beginning of Black Friday. When we arrived in Las Vegas later that evening, after checking in to our hotel, we began our excursion at Hard Rock Café before heading to the outdoor mall. The next morning, we woke up around ten o'clock and got ready to go, as we needed to check out of the hotel by eleven. We drove mostly in silence back to Flagstaff, tired and feeling those shopped-out blues.

In Flagstaff, Nichole was a waitress at Red Lobster. Brittany, Sarah, and I drove Nichole's car through the snow to have dinner there, and she waited on us. We got there safely, even though I was a bit scared driving on the icy roads while it was snowing. The next day, Nichole dropped the three of us off at the train station. With our pillows under our arms, we got on the train and headed home.

In December 2009, Nichole graduated from Northern

Arizona University! Our family, along with my parents, went to Flagstaff and celebrated with her, and we were joined there by Frank's family. It was quite chilly and snowing at the time. Again, I felt so distant from my oldest daughter, who, by the way, had a similar strong-willed personality as her dad, Norm.

I look back now and realize that I did not appreciate that personality trait in her or notice that it was part of what motivated her. It propelled her throughout her growing years, and now that she was married and a graduate from college, it would contribute to her success in her career. She had graduated from college in just two and a half years, as she had taken college courses in high school, as well as squeezing in some extra classes each year at NAU. She had ambition, and she had followed through with her goal to graduate from college the same year as Frank and continue their lives together.

Since I mentioned the snow during our Flagstaff girls trip, I realize that I forgot to write about all the family trips we took to Big Bear. Numerous times, our family rented cabins or stayed in my parents' time share. Our kids took ski lessons, and we all had fun seeing how many times we could take advantage of the crowded slopes and get in as many runs as possible. As they got a bit older, the kids would rather go on snowboards, while Norm and I continued skiing because the ski poles gave us a bit of added security to avoid falling!

We also enjoyed sledding, building snowmen, throwing snowballs, going on hikes or playing games indoors with the warmth from the fireplace, drying our boots and gloves. We rented a cabin from our friends each winter, and when possible, we brought our dog Holly with us. I think she loved the snow just as much as the lake. Our family also slid down on some large tires in the snow, and we had a blast, often riding with two of us per tire.

There were several times when Norm and I would take an

overnight or weekend excursion to the mountains and we stayed at a bed and breakfast. He did the planning and would make the reservations for our getaway. We would also ski together and go on walks, enjoying the scenery and just spending quality time with one another. Alone time was meaningful and priceless, and we took advantage of getting away by ourselves as our kids were growing up. On these trips alone, Norm did not seem as worried or stressed, and he was a lot more at ease.

# ⁓16⁓

## Expanding Balloon

In 2010, I began another chapter in life. I know God had His strong hand on my life's journey. Frank and Nichole had moved back to California a short time after she had graduated from college in December, the previous year. She began working as an accountant in Irvine, and they were living in Fullerton.

At the end of May 2010, for our twenty-fourth wedding anniversary, Norm and I took a short trip and stayed in San Juan Capistrano for a few days. We had brought our bikes with us, and we took a long ride on a bike trail with a view that overlooked the water and occasionally the freeway. As usual, we had a nice relaxing time away from home together, enjoying one another's company.

During the summer of 2010, Norm, Brittany, Sarah, and I all went on a trip to San Francisco. Brittany's soccer team had several tournaments during the time we stayed there, but in between soccer games, we made it a family trip touring San Francisco. We walked along a winding road called Lombard Street, went to the Ghirardelli Chocolate Factory, strolled through a movie star wax museum viewing all the amazing sculptures, and participated in other enjoyable tourist attractions, including of course, taking a ride on the famous trolley.

The new school year began in 2010, with our youngest daughter, Sarah, beginning high school at Valencia. I believe she was eager to get out of school and move on with her life from the first day of her high school years! Sarah was on the soccer team during the first two years of high school, mostly to meet her "two-year PE or sports participation" requirement for graduation. She continued taking art classes at studios and at Valencia, enjoying her talents as Mom showed it off.

Brittany was a junior at Valencia, keeping busy with soccer, cross country, and singing in the choir. It also was this year that she began dating a boy whom she had met through RDFC. They became boyfriend and girlfriend and were with each other all the time. He attended El Dorado High School (my alma mater), so they managed to have some time apart. She sang in the band onstage during church services while he played the drums, played the keyboard, or sang.

Bryan began his sophomore year at Cal State Fullerton. I believe it was this year when he met a professor whom I feel continued drawing Bryan even further away from his core Christian beliefs. It was very difficult for Norm and me to watch Bryan distance himself from his faith and from his relationship with his dad.

*In their hearts humans plan their course, but the Lord establishes their steps* (Proverbs 16:9).

In September, we happily celebrated my parents' fiftieth wedding anniversary with close and extended family members. The location of the party was at the Alta Vista Country Club in Placentia. This was the same location as our own wedding reception, twenty-four years prior. The club had been updated and redecorated, so it looked vastly different. During the party, we had many family photos taken by a photographer outdoors, all of us dressed in black and white attire.

Sometime during 2010, when Norm had his yearly EGD, we were told the results showed pre-cancerous polyps in his stomach, which the doctor, a specialist at Cedar Sinai, felt a little uneasy about. His stomach was inflated like a balloon, and Norm had to swallow a tiny camera, which then took an image of his stomach.

We had already once been down this road, facing the horrible possibility of Norm living without his colon and his stomach. We again decided to continue "walking in God's footprints" along life's trials and trusting in His path, as I tried my hardest to hold back the tears.

Later, in November, our family was informed that Mary, Norm's sister, was suffering again with cancer. It had returned from when she'd had it two years prior, in 2008. She had remarried, after being divorced for some time, to a man named Ken with whom she worked at George Key School. Norm, Brittany, Sarah, and I went over to Ken and Mary's home to celebrate Thanksgiving and saw Mary suffering from pain, due to the cancer that had now spread throughout her body.

I remember standing next to Norm and Mary in her bedroom, as Norm rubbed her back, trying to relieve some of her trauma in the areas where she felt the most pain. Not long after, on January 26, 2011, Mary passed away. Those feelings, emotions, and strain from all the pain, first that he had dealt with himself, followed by his mom, and now Mary, made a big impact on Norm this year.

The following verse relates to and defines the next five years I share in this book:

*Be strong and courageous. Do not be afraid or terrified because of them, for the Lord your God goes with you; he will never leave you nor forsake you* (Deuteronomy 31:6).

Toward the end of May 2011, Norm and I celebrated our twenty-fifth wedding anniversary. We spent several days away together, driving to Pismo Beach and staying at the Cottage Inn by the Sea. Norm always picked out special places for us to stay. We, of course, brought our bikes along with us on the trip and took a long coastal, scenic trail, which was enjoyable as usual.

On July 1, Sarah turned sixteen, so she went to look for a job and got her driver's license soon after. She first worked at Lascari's Italian Restaurant, then B.J.'s Pizza, and then she moved onto Macaroni Grill, where Bryan was also working at the time. Bryan had started working there when he began college. As you can pretty much tell, Sarah loved and still does love Italian food, especially pizza or my homemade lasagna.

A bit later in the summer of 2011, we went to Monterey, to check out Cal State Monterey. Before Brittany's senior year, she had been offered a scholarship at this college and she wanted to check out the soccer team. Norm, Brittany, Sarah, my parents, and I took a tour of the school. Her major was to be kinesiology, and she certainly wanted to play on the college soccer team.

After the interview with the coach at Monterey, he asked her to play on their team. But she eventually decided against moving and attending there. I believe this was mostly because she did not want to be that far away from her boyfriend, and second, their soccer team was the lowest in their ranking.

Another college Brittany was interested in was Cal State Los Angeles. Brittany, my mom, and I took a tour of the campus with a group leader, and while walking through campus, we each noticed a few signs stapled onto posts. The signs read: "A rapist seen on campus wanted!" That immediately helped us make a quick decision against this school.

Norm and I were able to check out another college, Cal State Pomona, with Brittany. We toured the campus a bit and watched Brittany, along with many other girls, try out for the soccer team. We all felt that she did well and were patiently waiting to hear back from the coach.

A few days later, she received a call that left her devastated. She had not been chosen as a member of the 2012 Cal State

Pomona team. She then decided, after a short amount of time passed, that she would enroll back at Cal State Fullerton and live at home, as Bryan had been doing for the past few years.

Of course, we still needed to take our good ol' boat on a family summer vacation. We chose to stay at my parents' Lake Havasu time share again. Audry, our niece, and Isaacia, her daughter, came along for the first part of the week. During our visit there at the condo, a monsoon-type storm occurred, and the five girls went outside to the back patio, dancing and humming to the lightning flashing above, just being their silly selves.

Throughout this past year, it seemed as though a monsoon storm had hit the Nortons' physical and emotional lifestyles.

# ～17～

# Up, Up in the Air

In September 2011, the new school year began, with Brittany in her last year of high school and Sarah closely following as a sophomore. Bryan was beginning his third year at Cal State Fullerton and still living at home. Norm and I planned a surprise birthday party for Brittany's eighteenth birthday.

We all met secretly at the Spaghetti Factory, and Brittany did seem surprised as she and Nichole entered the decorated room for the party. Family and friends all celebrated together, and I had a few of her memorable photo albums displayed of the busy, yet fun years of her in high school. In December, I planned another surprise birthday party, but this time for Norm and my sister, Sherrie, both who were turning fifty years old, five days apart.

During wintertime, Brittany's team, the Fullerton Rangers, had a soccer tournament that would be held at NAU in Flagstaff. I drove her there, along with my mom and Sarah, who was interested in visiting and touring the campus. It was quite cold sitting outside in the damp atmosphere, watching several soccer games whether they were in the morning, the afternoon, or the chillier evenings. Luckily, there was not any snow on the ground, but we bundled up and enjoyed watching the Fullerton Rangers win the tournament.

Continuing with soccer, the Valencia women's soccer team made it to CIF for the first time. Yahoo! The team and Coach Barry were extremely excited. We parents ran a close second with those feelings of happiness and elation. Brittany was so happy that the team was moving on to their final game in the CIF rounds, which was about two hours away. Unfortunately, Valencia lost this next game, and the girls along with the coaches and families were incredibly sad.

Brittany's high school soccer season ended with the last soccer banquet that she would participate in. Our good friend Coach Barry honored Brittany with "Player of the Year," and she was certainly Mom and Dad's top star on the field too! Besides that, she made some sneaky sliders during many games, swiping the ball from an opponent and executing many awesome passes to a player on her team or to make a goal.

In January 2012, I traveled with Norm to Puerto Rico on a business trip. As Norm would be attending meetings, going to conferences, and managing displays of the products he sold, I would be in our room working on family photo albums. Our room overlooked the sky and down on the Atlantic Ocean, which I viewed as I sat and made decorative pages with photos, stickers, and die cuts to add to each album. First thing in the mornings, though, I would bring a book I was reading downstairs, near the oceanfront, as I ate breakfast, drank coffee, and enjoyed the scenery.

Norm and I went shopping one day and drove around nearby. We did buy a hammock and hung it from the back patio at home in our backyard for many years. A few of my favorite memories of this trip was one evening, when Norm and I rested in a hammock looking up at a large palm tree, feeling buried with the moon and stars, as the ocean rolled ashore off to our side. Another evening, after picking up some cheese, meat, and crackers, we sat and ate on the sand, along the beach, each sipping our beer and watching the sunset.

Our twenty-sixth wedding anniversary rolled around at the end of May. After all the excitement was over at the end of the school year, with Brittany graduating from high school, we left on our extended weekend away. We had attached our bikes to the rack on the car and headed to Morro Bay, where we planned to stay at the Baywood Inn, which was across the street from the bay, quite cozy and quaint.

Norm had a bouquet of twenty-six pink roses waiting in the room when we arrived. He always bought me flowers "just because." On one of the evenings, we went to an outdoor dinner dance get-together with a live band. We walked around the area, ate, and then danced a little. On another day, we took a long bike ride exploring the surroundings of Morro Bay nearby.

We also went on a kayak adventure at Pismo Beach for our anniversary trip, which was supposed to be a "beginner's" tour. This was not the case! Well, the farther we were out on the ocean and closer to the rocks, the scarier it became. Waves became rougher against the rocks, and each of us on the kayak tour were told to drift through this enclosed, slim tunnel of rock formations, squeezing through while holding steadily onto our kayaks. After others went through, Norm followed along, but I was hesitant. I finally went for it, with Norm on the other side waiting and cheering me on.

Well, I fell off my kayak, into the water, and the man in charge came to rescue me as I was being pushed back and forth by the turbulence, close to the rocks on either side. I was scared that I would get pushed against a rock and hit my head, which certainly would not have been a good thing, due to my previous head injuries. The man lifted me out of the water and back onto the kayak, pushing me out of the narrow path in which I was stuck. That certainly scored as my least-favorite anniversary adventure that Norm and I had taken!

Sarah had previously chosen to sign up with a friend from church and school to volunteer for the summer at Quaker Meadow camp. Wow, my little girl going far away for about six weeks was an adjustment! She loved the outdoors, as she had often enjoyed hiking, and so now she would explore a new adventure on her own; but she was not alone for long. Sarah met Matt on her volunteer adventure.

When we headed on our family vacation to Oregon and picked up Sarah from Quaker Meadow, she introduced us to Matt. Quaker Meadow was approximately five hours away, so we had planned on picking her up on our trip heading to Oregon. When we arrived at the camp, we greeted Sarah with open arms, and soon after she said she would like to introduce us to a new friend she had met.

Norm, Brittany, and I followed Sarah as she led us to a building where there was an indoor rock-climbing wall. Matt had been assigned to help the climbers there, and she eagerly introduced us to him. We shook his hand, talked to him for a few minutes, and then we were off on our trip to Oregon.

Yes, our summer vacation was certainly different during 2012. We did not plan a boat trip to one of the many lakes we had explored in the past. Brittany and Sarah had mentioned months prior that they wanted to go on a different type of family vacation. They wanted our family to adventure to other places for new experiences. Because of this, Norm came up with the idea of traveling up the coast to Oregon, exploring different places along the way.

While driving on our long excursion, we all heard a lot about Sarah's new boyfriend, Matt. She told us that after she had met him, she did not really like him, but then she started to be attracted to his charm and personality later, as she got to know him.

Matt was staying as a volunteer worker the entire summer as he had done during previous summers. He was from Glendora, which was about twenty-five minutes away from our house, so I am sure we would be seeing him again when he returned home from camp.

We arrived in Lebanon, Oregon, where we stayed at Ken and Norma's home; Norma was Norm's sister. We were able to see Norm's dad, Norm Sr., while visiting, as he had moved in with Ken and Norma some time before.

Our family went to check out some waterfalls and venture on a hike, walking underneath the water flowing from above us and splashing far beneath us in the streams below. It was an awesome hike with beautiful sights. We stayed just a few days visiting them, and then we were headed to stay on the Rouge River.

We rented a hotel for one night about halfway to our final destination. This hotel was across the street from the river, so the girls took an adventure walking along the edge of the water, taking photos of each other with the scenic background.

In the morning, we drove farther to the south and stayed at another one of my parents' time share locations for a week. We pulled in, driving our large truck, with two kayaks and two canoes, tied to the top. We had purchased the canoes a while beforehand and borrowed two kayaks from Frank's parents. The place where we were staying was across the way from the ocean. I remember enjoying wild blackberries I was able to pick from the bushes in our so-called backyard.

More adventurous on our trip, we took a tour on a large boat, where we sat side by side, cruising the scenery on the Rogue River with other passengers on board. We viewed many beautiful creations God had placed on each side of the river. We did see, a few different times on the tour, large black bears as they were eating dead vultures in the broad daylight, while posing for the tourists' cameras.

Norm had brought his bike on the trip, so one day he decided to ride alone to a nearby city called Brookings, which was about thirty minutes away by car. The route had many narrow, climbing, and winding roads. While Norm was on his biking adventure, the three of us girls decided to drive and check out the so-called big and busy town of Brookings.

Well, as we finally found a supposed shopping center, there was only one store that carried all our necessities. This store reminded us of good old Kmart. I do not think we found much there to purchase as keepsakes, but we had a good laugh together when we compared it to the shopping centers or malls near our home in California.

We all decided to take a day out on the water with the kayaks, canoes, and Norm's fishing poles to have a relaxing day on the river. It did not end up as we had anticipated, as the winds were much too strong for us to manage rowing the kayaks and canoes in the water. It was quite turbulent also, which made it a bit difficult to begin with.

Norm told us all to head toward the shore, and as we did so, he then attached each of the kayaks and canoes together with ropes, one behind another. It was a fun idea at first until we lost strength in our arms after working so hard to move against the current. When we returned to the shore, Norm removed the ropes and we stored everything back on the truck. On the way back to our place, we took a beautiful drive through the pretty green scenery, down narrow roads, until we arrived at a stream nearby.

On one of our last days there, we drove again to the city of Brookings, but first we stopped on our way along the ocean and climbed on many rocks. Earlier we had made horseback riding reservations for that afternoon. After we put on helmets and climbed onto our horses, we were ready for another adventure. A trail guide led us toward the ocean, riding our horses through the sand, just in time for a gorgeous sunset. It was a very pretty sight to see and was well worth the experience!

In the fall of 2012, Brittany would be starting college at Cal State University Fullerton. She was on the intermural soccer team for CSUF, which was not the demanding, competitive, or time-consuming team she was used to. She still had weekly practices, and she played many games against opposing teams, which we enjoyed watching for fun. Bryan was in his fourth year at CSUF, and Sarah was beginning her junior year at Valencia and now had a boyfriend, Matt.

Matt played on the softball team through the church he attended, Glendora Friends. They played against other Friends church teams, including RDFC, where we attended. I went with Sarah to one of his games and met Matt's parents.

It was at this game that Ron, a man we had known for quite some time from church, came up to me and asked if Norm and I would be interested in joining their Care Group Bible study. I said I would talk with Norm, and soon we joined this special group of people who became family. I am still part of that blessed Care Group today!

I believe at that time, Frank and Nichole were renting a home off Eureka Avenue, close by us in Yorba Linda. The home was around fifty years old. They now had a backyard for their dog to run around and play in, and they probably thoroughly enjoyed living on their own in a larger place.

During this same year, my niece Audry had her colon removed, as she, too, had previously been diagnosed with Familia Polyposis. She was just over thirty years old, and she decided it was the right time to have it removed before the polyps found inside her colon turned to cancer. Her surgery was performed at Hoag Hospital in Newport Beach.

In December, we began a new Christmas tradition with a few others from our Care Group. We were going to bring blankets, socks, clothing, and cards with a check enclosed to the homeless. Norm knew the areas quite well where there were many homeless, as this was where he often rode his bike along the nearby bike trails.

We gathered and went to hand out these needed items to those people on the sides of bike paths, in parks, and near the train stations. We spoke to them and prayed with them, and it was such a meaningful time, especially for Norm, as he could very closely relate to those same trials, he had many years ago at a young age.

The last thing I remember from 2012 was that Norm and I went to Utah again to the Huntsman Cancer Research Center, as he was accepted to undergo another clinical trial as he had previously done, years in the past. This time they would check his stomach along with his rectum. In this trial, they viewed, removed, and ran biopsies on many of the polyps that were discovered, none of which were found in the rectum.

This was a good result, because if any had been found in the rectum, it would had been quite difficult, if not impossible, to remove them. The doctor did not see anything that looked like cancer, and I specifically remember the doctor telling Norm that he needed to continue to have the polyps in his stomach checked once a year.

Later in 2013, during the school year, Sarah participated in her first clinical trial as Norm had in the past. She was just seventeen years old. For this clinical trial she would have a colonoscopy and an EGD done at the same place, Huntsman Cancer Hospital and Research Center in Salt Lake City. She and I planned a trip together to Utah for a few days, just the two of us.

It all went well, as she did not have to take the same terrible prep drink as she had done in the past. Sarah simply took a few pills and could only drink Gatorade or water on the day of the procedure. They removed polyps, like they had done in the past, found in her colon and her stomach. They also ran biopsies to make sure there was no cancer, and soon after, they found that the polyps were all negative.

The great thing about these trials, besides the easy prep and the quick results, was that they did not cost us a dime. They paid for our travel and our stay there in the hotel on campus, at the research center. As I wrote in the title of this chapter, this Familia Polyposis would be an ongoing trial within the Norton family.

# ⬾18⬿

# Holding Life's Anxiety

With all these situations, including the clinical trials, gastroenterologist appointments, surgery, and other medical concerns dealing with extended family, I suppose I should begin my next chapter. We were still walking on this journey, trying to figure out where God was leading us at this time in our lives. Norm constantly was quietly thinking about why this was all happening to him and our family, while his anxiety was increasing.

I began reminding him about the verses in the Bible that I viewed differently, I am sure, than how he did. This was because he was the one undergoing the physical and spiritual pain of this ongoing disease. Norm's faith was the strongest in our family and among his extended family members, yet he seemed frustrated, keeping hold of his emotions, confused, and afraid for his future, along with our family's future and the dreams he had for himself.

*Humble yourselves, therefore under God's mighty hand, that he may lift you up in due time. Cast all your anxiety on him because he cares for you* (1 Peter 5:6–7).

A few months passed, and it was May, time to celebrate our twenty-seventh anniversary. We decided to spend a few days in Ventura at a bed and breakfast that had previously been an old church. It had been redone into several bedrooms, a kitchen, dining room, and a room where guests could relax.

Norm had done research ahead of time and planned out our

following day. We were going to boat over to Anacapa Island with others and explore. We had our lunch packed ahead of time, and off we went for our adventurous day.

It turned out that there was not much to see on this island. It took a large amount of time from when we all were dropped off by the boat before it returned to take us back to shore. While on Anacapa Island, everyone went their own way. This was the second least favorite adventure from our many anniversary trips.

If you recall, my first least-favorite was the time we went on the scary kayak trip at Pismo Beach. Anyway, Norm and I were hot and bored, and to top it off, Norm was pooped on by one of the many seagulls continuously flying overhead. We tried to dodge them, but one got Norm right in the center of his forehead. Luckily, we had a spare napkin from our lunch to clean it off the best we could. The next day, before heading home, we rode our bikes along the beach boardwalk. This I enjoyed a lot more than our day before on that swarming seagull island!

As the school year grew closer to an end, Sarah began thinking more and more about finishing high school and moving on to college sooner than waiting another year. She and I had done some research on it, and we decided to enroll her in La Entrada High School, where she would finish off and receive her high school diploma.

This would require her to keep up with her studying, reading, learning, and doing homework independently at home. She would go to La Entrada to take tests on the material each week of her enrollment. They interviewed her, looked at her previous grades, and accepted her to accomplish this on her own, beginning the next school year.

July 1 was coming up, and I was planning on throwing a surprise party for Sarah for her eighteenth birthday. I had given each one of our other kids a surprise birthday celebration at either their sixteenth or eighteenth birthdays. Sarah insisted that I did not surprise her; she wanted us to throw a party for her at The Spaghetti Factory, one of her favorite restaurants. I planned it with decorations, along with the display of her photo albums with all her high school memorabilia.

Also, during the summer, Brittany planned to go on a girls' missionary trip to Japan for two weeks. Several months before the trip, she had heard about the organization called Southern California Seahorse Soccer. She had played soccer with this Christian soccer team when she was younger.

On the Seahorse soccer trip, Brittany and the team were terribly busy playing continuous soccer daily in the hot humidity in Japan. She was happy to return to California, but she had a good time there being a witness of her faith and having much practice playing soccer.

Norm, our family summer vacation planner, made reservations at Lake Shasta in August 2013. We had invited my mom and dad to join us and had made reservations in a small cabin at a place called Sugar Loaf Cottages, which was walking distance to the lake. We towed our boat with the truck, so my parents had to drive separately. My dad brought along our two canoes inside of the back of his large van. Brittany invited her boyfriend to join us, and Sarah had invited Matt.

We were all extremely excited for our vacation plans, not realizing this would be our last time out with Norm's favorite family boat. We took off for our long trip, arriving at Lake Shasta. The atmosphere was gorgeous, with an overabundance of tall, green trees along with deer near the cottages where we were staying. Our good old dog Holly enjoyed every minute of exploring the scenery and playing ball, especially in the lake.

We had such memorable times with my parents on this trip. I remember how much fun most of us had playing Mexican Train. I said "most of us," since my father and Norm were the ones who would rather watch TV, read, or fall asleep in the lounge chairs while the rest of us laughed away, trying to win this fun-filled entertaining game each night for hours on end!

My parents joined us a few times to go along on our busy boat excursions. My mom loved the water, and as a passenger, she watched all the kids ride on the wake boards, tubes, and knee boards, and then there was me, who just rode on my wide water skis. That was just fine for me. We cheered for the kids and laughed with them being their adventurous selves in the water.

One day, Brittany, Sarah, and their boys wanted to explore a hike they could get to, a bit of a distance away, from where we would relax and wait for them on the boat. We all piled in the boat, along with my mom and dad and Holly, and headed for the cove, where we dropped the anchor. The kids got out of the boat and began their hike, heading up onto the mountain nearby, as we adults hung out on the boat and ate our packed lunches.

Meanwhile, I suggested that my mom and I go for a dip in the lake next to the boat. It turns out that she was afraid to go into the water. After I convinced her to put on a life preserver, my dad and I helped her down the boat ladder, and once in the water, we assured her we would stay next to the boat. My dad kept a close eye on her while sitting in the boat.

Mom then told me she never had learned how to swim, but she was not afraid of her pool at home if she stayed in the shallow end. We both had fun laughing and floating near the boat. After a bit, Norm swam over to help me get her back on the boat, with Dad lifting her up onboard. The kids had returned from their hike, and we headed the boat back to its parking space near the cottages.

One of the days we adventured to Shasta Caverns, where we took a long, winding tour to explore the inside of the caverns. There were many steps going through, so we took our time walking slowly, since my mom needed to take many rests after climbing up each set of stairs along the way. We all enjoyed the beauty of nature and the way it had been preserved and kept clean.

Later during our vacation week, Norm seemed to be in a frustrated, uptight mood, which had continually happened during other vacations. This was happening more and more as the kids were getting older. Since he had brought along his bike, he took off and went for a long ride into the wilderness.

Most of the times when Norm became really bothered or upset, he would bite his tongue with an angry, ready-to-blow-up type of expression. He would not say anything about the issue or situation that had upset him. For me or anyone who noticed this, we just let it pass and moved on with the day. Norm would rather not express his innermost feelings, most of the time.

We left to head back home the next day, and there were more changes to come in our family dynamic at home. Bryan began his last year at Cal State Fullerton before graduating and decided it was time to move out of our home, where he had grown up. He had met a friend through school, and they rented an apartment right across the street from the college. We helped him move his furniture and belongings and watched him as he was heading more in a solid direction, starting with his independence.

Brittany was beginning her second year at Cal State Fullerton, and she still played on the intermural soccer team at the college. A bit into the school year, she and her boyfriend decided to break up after two years of dating. I know that must have been difficult for Brittany, as this was her first true love.

This school year, Sarah was going to begin her studies at La Entrada. She kept up with her independent studies, went in to take the tests once a week, and finished her senior year in six weeks! Wow, she had perseverance and motivation like Nichole, getting it done quickly, and then moving on to the next step in furthering her career. Kind of sounds like her dad as well, huh?

Sarah had looked at various schools within the past year, and my mom and I had taken her to tour Laguna College of Art and Design, as this was her first choice. After seeing how competitive the college was, the income she could make if she were to graduate and succeed in art, and the price it would be to attend, she began to think more on using her art talent as a hobby, instead of as a career major.

Sarah decided to choose nursing as a major and continue her artistic talent as a side job. Norm and I had taken her on a tour of UC Berkley, while Brittany had a weekend soccer tournament nearby. I had also gone with her to check into Azusa University, where she had an interview to receive a potential scholarship. Thinking of the price she would have to pay, even with her scholarship, she chose Northern Arizona University, which we had toured in 2012. She would work toward a nursing major there.

NAU was where Nichole had attended, and so another child of ours was going to attend college quite a distance away the following year. This college was less expensive than the other ones she was interested in. Norm had told her, as he had with our previous kids, that we could only afford the amount of a state school and living at home. She was eager, again like Nichole, and she would set those plans for the following year.

April 2014 was approaching, and yes, I was going to be turning fifty years old! Norm planned to have a surprise birthday party for me at Don Jose's Restaurant, and the kids followed through with all the party details and invites. I had the feeling something was being planned, but I acted surprised as I entered, with friends and family there to celebrate. I remember my dad giving a toast regarding my recovery since my 1984 car accident, and all the progress I had made in life in the past thirty years.

In May, Bryan graduated from Cal State Fullerton after a long, hard, stressful five years of studying. He received a diploma stating, "In Recognition of Outstanding Scholarship," and on the following line it read, "Honors Convocation," and it finished with stating, "Summa Cum Laude." In other words, as his mom, this meant to me that he had accomplished wonderful work with his smart little mind and was eagerly moving forward toward his future goals and career. His majors were English and philosophy.

We had a large party to celebrate at our home, with many friends and family. Of course, I had a few of his mementos from times during his most recent years displayed in photo albums for others to look at. He had decided to move to Los Angeles for a year with his friend, where he would work and explore, taking a year off from college before pursuing his master's degree.

We helped him move into an apartment in Echo Park, which was a decent area, and soon after, he got a job at an expensive restaurant in downtown LA. Bryan no longer had a car, so he was riding his bike to and from work, rain or shine, or taking the bus to get around. He enjoyed this busy, crowded, hectic lifestyle, and he was happy living again on his own.

At the end of May in 2014, Norm and I celebrated our twenty-eighth wedding anniversary. He planned our anniversary trip for a stay on the Queen Mary. This is where we had gone on our second date for the day, many years ago. On this anniversary trip, we had a lot of fun riding our bikes around Long Beach, cruising by the entrance of the ports where he was selling his products for work. We continued our ride to Dana Point on our bikes and went on the Auqalink, which was a catamaran used as a water taxi.

We had another graduation in June, this one for Sarah, our last child to graduate from high school. Our family, grandparents, and Matt were all at the ceremony, cheering for her accomplishments. We happened to find ourselves each clapping continuously, as she received an award in each category with top honors. We were so proud of her!

Brittany had made the decision again to join another missionary trip this year. In the summer of 2014, she raised money for a mission trip to Ireland. This was through Reign Ministries, and she was off on her next expedition. Brittany seemed to enjoy this trip a lot. They played a little soccer, but they spent more time sharing the Gospel and making close friends with girls she traveled with and with people living in Ireland.

After seeing the success of all four of our kids, growing up and becoming independent adults, even though I did not want to let go, I now see that it was a major stepping-stone both for them and for us as their parents.

*"For I know the plans I have for you," declares the Lord, "plans to prosper you and not to harm you, plans to give you hope and a future"* (Jeremiah 29:11).

# ≈19≈

## Sharing Faith and Prayer

Summertime was going by fast, and Norm had planned a vacation to Costa Rica with Brittany, Sarah, and me. Nichole and Frank had been there in the past for a friend's wedding, and they said it was a lot of fun, so we decided to check it out. Norm had found, through Home Away from Home, a two-story house to rent for ten days that was right across the street from the ocean.

We arrived there at the beginning of August, rented a car in the main city of Jaco, and stopped off at a fruit and vegetable stand, which was often seen along the dirt roads. We were all in awe of how large the rooms were. There was plenty of space, with our room downstairs and the girls' room upstairs. Out on the upstairs patio, adjacent to the living room and kitchen, were two hammocks looking out onto the ocean with overflowing, tall hazel-green trees trailing into the backyard by the pool.

This house had all the necessities for our family, including surfboards, boogie boards, and beach towels. It was close to the beach, and there was also a hired outdoor guard who sat outside on the front patio each night. His job was to stay alert for anyone or anything that might happen to approach the property. Funny thing was, though, each night he would fall asleep while sitting in a chair out front as our watchman.

We welcomed the guard to join us for dinner a few nights on the patio, and one day he grabbed hold of an iguana for each of the girls to hold by the pool. There were many iguanas wandering peacefully around out back. He also cleaned the pool several times and captured any loose frogs in the pool, which often entered at nighttime.

It was quite scary returning at night, though, as we walked to the door, which was in the back near the pool. We had to keep an eye out for crabs in the grass that had crawled from the nearby ocean. They happened to be scattered all among the grass area, and there was little light surrounding the home at night so we could barely see them. Fortunately, we managed never to be grabbed by a crab.

During our trip, Norm had his usual frustration about making plans to enjoy our trip sightseeing, rather than just hang out at the place where we rented. Without much enthusiasm, he found some places for entertainment. Our first adventure was to explore more nature on the Crocodile Tour. We coasted along the water in a small boat with others, viewing crocodiles onshore and nearby. They were so close we could have reached out from the boat and touched them.

Another day we took a long nature hike through Manuel Antonio National Park and ended up at the ocean. Here we were surrounded with many wild little monkeys, who acted quite social as one decided to hang from a tree behind where Sarah was standing and take her snack right out of her hand! A few times we drove to Jaco, a nearby city about thirty minutes away. We shopped around, and of course, Brittany and I had to check out their iced coffee lattes each time in this tiny town.

Back at our rental home, we took advantage of the surf and boogie boards and took them for a swim in the ocean. As Norm and Sarah rode the boogie boards, Brittany attempted to surf, although the waves were extremely rough. I enjoyed watching a beautiful sunset and seeing my family having fun in the ocean. I was just fine staying warm on shore, avoiding the crabs crawling up from the sand.

On our next day, we went on another hike with a tour guide

to reach the spot where we individually grabbed onto zip-lines and soared on six to eight different flying adventures, with beautiful sights everywhere we looked. We enjoyed this a lot, and that was my first ride on a zip-line. I will never forget that experience! After our zip-line adventure, we ended up at a waterfall before a tiring hike back to the starting point.

We had gone out to eat dinner one evening, and on our way back, both Brittany and Sarah hung out of the car windows in the back seat. As we were driving slowly near our rental, Norm spontaneously began to head toward each crab he saw in the headlights of our car. We captured some fun moments, as he purposely attempted to smash each crab he saw with the tires. When we all heard a large crunch on the ground, the girls cheered for more. That was a memorable time where we all had some fun laughs together, doing something silly.

Another day we went on a kayak tour, stopped off at a beach, halfway on the journey, and were given some fresh pineapple to eat. We needed some fuel to give us energy, as we then prepared to go snorkeling. We saw and touched large, colorful puffed fish, and then we all headed back on the kayaks, getting dried off by the sunshine.

That evening, Norm planned to go on an excursion by himself. He took a bucket and some tongs from the barbeque pit out back, determined to capture several crabs crawling out front on the street at night. Norm caught many and took the time to barbecue them and offer each of us a gourmet crab to try for lunch the following day. Sarah and I tasted them as Dad served them on the patio, but we did not like the small little creatures. However, Norm and Brittany enjoyed every morsel and ate them all, finding them quite scrumptious!

The day before we left our lovely rental, we went on a mangrove boat ride. On this tour, the driver of the boat brought us back into a small jungle, where we saw many more baby monkeys hanging in the trees. We were handed some small chunks of food to feed to the monkey's tiny mouths. It was quite entertaining, and the monkeys seem to enjoy it also.

The summer of 2014 was almost over, and it was August, time to celebrate my dad and sister Laura's birthdays. Laura was turning forty-eight, and my dad was turning seventy-five years old, so I planned a surprise party for his big seventy-fifth birthday at The Spaghetti Factory. Dad was surprised, and we had a good time celebrating.

In September, Norm's father, Norm Sr., decided to move in with us. He had been living with Norm's sister Norma in Oregon. He had spoken to Norm before and told him that he wanted to move back to a warmer climate. That was a big adjustment for all of us, and it did not look like Norm and I would have an empty nest for quite some time.

Brittany was still living at home. She was working as an aide to children with autism, as I had done, and attending her third year at Cal State Fullerton. Sarah was preparing to move out of our home soon and head to Arizona, where she would begin her first year at NAU. When that time came, I was in tears, driving my second daughter to a school so far away. Norm, Matt, and I moved Sarah into her dorm and enjoyed our time with one another for a few days. We walked around campus, and I remember heading to our car on the last day. We said good-bye after hugging each other tightly while trying to hold back tears.

During the month of October, we noticed that Holly, our golden retriever, had been getting very weak and lethargic, so we took her in to be tested. The doctors found out that she had cancer in her esophagus and was having a difficult time swallowing. We knew we could not afford the expense of surgery, and because Holly was close to eleven years old, we simply kept her as comfortable as possible. On October 31, Holly was put to sleep, with Norm and me right by her side. That was an awfully hard time in seeing someone close to us die.

In November, Sarah came home to visit one weekend and wanted to check out places to purchase a new puppy for the Norton household. Against Norm's opinion on the matter of getting another dog, Brittany, Sarah, and I went to Petco on a Saturday close to Thanksgiving to look at rescue dogs. We were the first ones there, waiting for the store to open. I believe it was Sarah who first saw a cute, little black puppy, that looked a lot like our old dog, Shasta, when she was a puppy.

We all held her, and of course, immediately fell in love with this little black, mixed-breed ball of fur! She would be ready for pickup in about a week or so, and this would be our next addition and wonderful Christmas gift for the Norton family! When Bryan came home from Los Angeles to visit, he came up with the name Harper for the new puppy.

Christmastime was here, and our new puppy, Harper, was our entertainment. I do remember a gift my kids put together for me that Christmas that was quite funny and original. They went to a grocery store, tore off many of the hanging coupons in the aisles, taped them together, and then put them in my stocking. Yes, they were making fun of my weekly shopping habits, as I tried to save our family every penny I could, using a variety of coupons. I laughed as it slowly appeared as I pulled it out of my stocking!

One afternoon in April, Brittany showed me a photo on her phone of a guy she had recently met at a coffee shop in Fullerton. She had asked me if I thought he was cute. The guy's name was Brandon, and he attended Biola University and had a common interest with Brittany in soccer. Brandon and Brittany began to spend time together and build a relationship with one another.

It was now May 2015, time to celebrate our twenty-ninth anniversary. Norm and I went to explore Seattle, Washington, and we stayed in a bed and breakfast Norm had found online. It was a quaint, country-style home. Of course, there was a condition behind our free travel deal offered by his company on our anniversary. Norm would have to spend some time working on the side, going to the ports, and meeting with customers there.

The bed and breakfast seemed a bit uncomfortable and awkward to me. We had a bedroom upstairs in the corner, yet the restroom was located down the hallway—NOT adjacent to our room. I did not find it very comfortable, as I packed up my necessities in the morning to shower, with makeup, hairdryer, brush, and a change of clothes, and at nighttime, for washing my face, brushing my teeth, etc.

Another episode that bothered me was that each morning, Norm would wake up, get dressed, and then proceed downstairs for coffee. He would then either read, get on his laptop, or begin socializing with the others in the dining area. At the same time, I would still be awake in bed, but Norm had no interest in cuddling or being romantic or talking with me at that time. This certainly made me feel lonely and sad, but I did not share with him how it deeply bothered me, and this was not the first time it happened on our getaways together.

Anyway, enough of my complaining and onto the fun times we did have in Seattle. We stayed on the outskirts of the big city, and we took a shuttle to explore the happening places. First, we walked among the crowds, for a long day viewing the large, well-known city, and then we strolled by fisherman's wharf.

We took a ferry one evening over to an island for dinner at a Mexican restaurant, and on our return, we observed the beautiful, bright lights of Seattle onshore. Another day, in between Norm's working schedule, we stood with a pack of tourists in line to go onto the Skyline, which again overlooked the city. We celebrated our anniversary eating dinner at a quaint little Italian restaurant called Che Sara Sara.

I believe it was during the summer of 2015 that Frank and Nichole purchased their first home. Yes, they were farther away from their hometown, but they were so pleased about a place to call home. It was a two-story duplex in San Juan Capistrano. Norm and I were happy for them and for their future ahead.

The end of August came, and it was time for another family vacation for the Norton clan. Norm had made plans to reserve my parents' timeshare in Kauai. I had never been to this island before, and we were all quite excited to go. I was happy that Bryan joined us on our family trip this time, as he had not done so in the past several years. Also, Matt, Sarah's boyfriend, came along, so we shoved a family of six into a two-bedroom condo.

I remember taking a walk each brisk morning. The walkway was along the ocean, as our time share was located right across from this picturesque sight. I always walked alone, because Norm never wanted to join me, and the kids loved to sleep in. I missed not having my "other half" on these walks each morning, as I was thinking and praying every step of the way.

All of us agreed that our most favorite Kauai adventure was going on a hike surrounded by nature. The trail we followed ended with a view down from a hill at Queen's Bath. This was the spotlight of gorgeous waterfalls, overlooking Princeville Coves, which had a splendid, refreshing area for swimming.

Our kids all took advantage of jumping from a cliff, next to the waterfall, into the majestic, clear water below. We also went sightseeing on hikes to the Kilauea Lighthouse and Waimea Canyon, which ended at Pio Pu Beach, where we dove into the water and went snorkeling. We came across so many bright, colorful fish and gigantic, swimming turtles.

Later in the week, Brittany reminded us that she felt determined to catch a wave, surfing in the famous Hawaiian ocean. Norm and I, along with Sarah and Brittany, found a place to rent a surfboard and a few boogie boards, and we headed to the beach. The waves were quite strong, along with the wind, so I just sat on the beach and watched them all.

Toward the last part of our busy expedition exploring Kauai, we went to Glass Beach. It was comprised of many small pieces of various shapes and different colors of glass that had rolled in from old ships, long ago. The glass particles were said to have been from treasure boxes dumped overboard. It was breathtaking to see!

We were all extremely exhausted after a long, busy week. I cannot help but mention again that several different times during our family vacation, Norm showed tension and was short-tempered. He did not want to talk with me about what was wrong. Inside my heart, I believed his stress with work and the worry of spending money were overtaking his freedom to have fun, more so during family vacation times. The kids had noticed this too on past vacations, especially as they grew older.

*But seek first his kingdom and his righteousness, and all these things will be given to you as well. Therefore do not worry about tomorrow, for tomorrow will worry about itself. Each day has enough trouble of its own* (Matthew 6:33–34).

During the summertime, Brittany and Brandon began seeing each other on a regular basis. He lived with his family in Chino Hills and was attending a church in Fullerton called For His Glory. Brittany had been spending a large part of her time and fellowship with Rose Drive Friends Church throughout her life. In September, there were some big moves. First, Brittany decided to begin attending the church where Brandon went.

Also, this month, Bryan was on the move to Germany again, yet this time for an entire year. He was heading to Koln, a small area, and he planned on attending the University of Koln. Bryan was eager to experience Germany and study the German language, while attending University of Koln on a full scholarship/grant!

Toward the end of 2015, I asked my mom if she would like

to begin doing a devotion together from *The Daily Bread*. We had made it a weekly ritual every Saturday to take walks at the park. She was interested, so we sat in the sunshine facing the lake in my truck, both taking turns reading the devotion and verses from the Bible. We then wrote down and shared some prayer requests and praises in a journal. Each time we shared together our feelings, Mom would begin to tear up, either out of happiness from being together or for the praises and prayer requests mentioned. It was quite a special time sharing with her, and afterward, we would begin our walk around the lake a few times.

Christmastime had arrived again, but it certainly was different without Bryan joining us for our usual traditions. He was welcomed, though, to celebrate with Anton's family. It made us happy to know that he would be joining them and was not alone on Christmas, so far away. We were invited to celebrate at Frank and Nichole's new home in San Juan Capistrano. Little did I know, this Christmas with our family together would be a lasting memory to cherish.

# ≈20≈

## Seeing the Unseen

Speaking of memories, 2016 turned into a year I will never forget, which starts the next chapter in my life. It began with a trip to Germany, so we could visit and travel with Bryan. This trip was an early thirtieth-anniversary celebration, and again, Norm's employer helped pay for flights and reservations for our stay at several of the different places we explored. In turn, Norm was committed to doing some business with companies while in Germany.

We came across a Coffee Bean on our walk near the hotel, which was very convenient for my coffee habit. Norm and I went in, and after placing our order, we sat looking out the window, thinking of our week ahead. After our coffee, we checked into our room at the hotel, City Class Hotel, and were greeted warmly, before we met Bryan for dinner nearby.

As I entered the room, directly in front of me was a spiral staircase, and lying on the counter at the top was a bouquet of dozen roses from Norm for our thirtieth anniversary. We laughed together after seeing the wilted flowers, but I was still thankful for Norm's thoughtfulness.

The room was immaculate, and through our slanted windows, we had a clear view of the Cathedral of Koln, more beautiful when it was lit up at nighttime. We were so excited to see Bryan our first night there, as we met for pizza. It was great seeing him, since it had been about six months since he had left for Germany.

The following day, Thursday, we toured the cathedral close by, and then we went to Romisch Germanisches Museum, which was a museum of Roman artifacts and antiques of the Roman Empire. We walked along the Rhine River nearby, and then we ended our evening with dinner at a German restaurant, where we tried the famous German beer.

On Friday, the three of us traveled on a train to visit the University of Koln, where Bryan was enrolled. He brought us to his office there, which he shared with the professor, Stephan, whom he worked under. Bryan had been accepted to the University of Pennsylvania for a full-ride scholarship the following year. This was granted to him for six years, as he worked on his PhD in German comparative literature.

On Saturday, we began our further adventures, leaving Koln and driving south to Heidelberg. This was one of my favorite places in Germany, as it was breathtaking. We first stopped off at a quaint restaurant and tried the falafel wraps, which were delicious.

Norm, Bryan, and I then walked over the long, wide, decorative Karl Theodor Bridge overlooking the Neckar River. Sunday arrived, our fourth full day in Germany, and we hiked in a downpour of rain to the Heidelberg Castle, up on a hill. The tour was spectacular with a great view overlooking the city, which I enjoyed under an umbrella I shared with Bryan.

On Sunday afternoon, we began driving south to Freidburg. By the time we arrived, it was early evening, and most of the streets were covered with streams of water about twelve inches wide or so, flowing to infinity, bordered on each side by the sidewalk. The belief behind this subtle, widespread décor was that "if you fall in one, you will marry a Freidburg." This brought a laugh to each of us.

For our next adventure, we journeyed through the Black Forest to Titisee. We stopped off on the side of the windy road on our way through the mountains, and took some photos standing in the cold, brisk snow. The small town of Titisee was a quaint area where the famous cuckoo clocks originated.

On Monday evening, we drove east to Zirndorf, where we stayed overnight. After checking in, we found only one restaurant open in yet another tiny town, and so we hurried in before they closed. Bryan taught us the German beer toast called "Prost," where you do cheers with the mugs and stare deeply into one another's eyes.

Early Tuesday morning, we headed to Prague, Czech Republic, which Bryan had previously told us he would like to explore on our vacation together. We saw, among many other attractions, a "World Clock" that stood out, as we listened to it chime on the hour.

This same day, we walked along a stunning sight called Charles Bridge. On this bridge, there were many landmarks of Jesus and His crucifixion, along with people selling items and homeless neighbors with coin cans held out. Prague was a busy, historical atmosphere that really caught our attention.

On Wednesday, we toured the emotional Jewish Holocaust Museum and Cemetery. On the walls inside were many plaques, reaching from ceiling to the floor, with millions of people's names who were killed by the Nazis during World War II. In another room were several pictures on the wall, drawn by children in the concentration camps, whose fathers were away at war.

The next day was Thursday, and we walked on a long, climbing journey up a hill to visit the Franz Kafka Museum. After this, we viewed the outside of Prague Castle, and we went inside and toured St. Nicholas Cathedral, where we were astounded by the architectural talent throughout. We walked by several other small exhibits, and at one exhibit, Norm payed for each of us to have three tries shooting at a target. Norm hit the bullseye, Bryan ran a close second, and I came in last place!

On the same day, we headed out on another extended walk. We reached our destination at the viewpoint overlooking the entire city of Prague. The view was remarkable.

Walking back toward the exit of the park, we saw a homeless man sitting on a bench. Norm, Bryan, and I decided to stop and chat with him. Norm did most of the talking, and after walking away from the man, he suggested we go to a store nearby, purchase some food and drinks, and then bring the items back to this man on the bench. We did so and prayed with him.

Friday arrived, and we were on our way leaving Prague and heading to Hertzberg. After several hours of a scenic drive, we arrived at Anton's house, who welcomed us with open arms. We happily met his dad and mom. We also met Anton's grandma and brother. There was much talking going on in Russian, German, and English, with all the excitement.

Anton's mother and grandmother both were our "chefs" for three meals a day for us all, which, come to find out, was their usual routine. It felt as if we had always sat at their kitchen table, eating and talking nonstop in three languages, as Anton interpreted for everyone present. We had many laughs with the Berg family, especially at mealtime.

Saturday was our last day of traveling, before we headed back to Koln. First, though, before leaving Herzberg, Anton's mom, Anton, Bryan, Norm, and I rode to Goslar. We walked along infinite cobblestones, exploring reminiscent buildings dating back to the 1200s. After several hours of touring, we headed back to their home, where we said our farewells and returned to Koln.

It was wonderful to see Anton and finally meet his family. I was so glad that he and Bryan were staying in touch. We sadly said good-bye, and Bryan headed back to his place in Koln, while Norm and I prepared to leave the following day to return to California.

I cannot help but share some feelings and observations as a

side note about this exhilarating and meaningful trip to Germany. I began noticing on the first morning we awoke in Germany that Norm had less energy. It was more noticeable in the evening. He was not getting up earlier than me and leaving our room before I was ready, as he often did on previous trips. On this trip, he told me that he would rather sleep in more, since we were on vacation. This just did not seem like the Norm I knew from our many past vacations or romantic anniversary trips.

I do recall specifically mentioning to him our first morning there that, when we returned home, he should make a doctor's appointment and have his stomach checked. It had been nearly four years since he had done so. He said, as he had several times in the past few years, that he wasn't going back to see a doctor to have another EGD done. If he did end up getting cancer, then he would get cancer!

Also, during our visit there, at various times Norm was more stressed and uptight than usual about spending money. His relationship with Bryan also seemed continuously on edge. Norm and I did not discuss what bothered him; he kept his feelings to himself, and I let it go.

Another noticeable difference was that Norm stayed behind on a few sightseeing adventures, as he said his right leg was hurting. This had been an issue for him several times when he rode his bike in the past during many excursions. He acted like it was no big deal and chalked it up to being out of shape. I shrugged it off, although it was continually on my mind. I tried to be joyful and interested in our time with Bryan.

# ⪩21⪨

## Step-by-Step Challenges

Sometime after our trip during the late spring of 2016, Norm finally decided to go to the doctor and address back pain he had been experiencing. Between April and June, he saw three different doctors. The first appointment was with his primary doctor, who was familiar with Norm's medical history. His diagnosis was "stress."

A bit later, he went to get another doctor's opinion, because the pain did not go away. This second doctor had another miraculous "cure" for the pain: Norm was to wear a waist wrap for back support, to help with the tension that might be caused by fatigue or extra weight. The pain continued, until a third doctor advised Norm to sit in a more comfortable desk chair when he leaned over at home on his computer.

As time passed, Norm quickly began losing weight. I was a little worried, but he said he was just trying to eat less, thinking this might help his aches and pains. Because he adjusted his workspace at home, lost weight, and continued to wear his waist wrap, Norm began to feel better.

While we were attempting to address Norm's pain issues, we officially celebrated our thirtieth anniversary in May 2016. We stayed at my parents' time share at the Welk's Resort in Escondido, and we brought our bikes along. As we drove toward San Diego, we stopped off at Crystal Cove and had lunch at Beachcomber, one of my favorite restaurants, located right on the beach.

The next day, we rode our bikes down to the beach in Escondido and then along the boardwalk. On our last day, we decided to drive to Oceanside. From there, we took a bike ride to Carlsbad and back, which was approximately fifteen miles each way. We had lunch in Carlsbad, and I had an enjoyable time riding bikes with the beautiful, offshore scenery of the beach.

While eating lunch, Norm looked it up and found that he had earned enough points on his membership card from traveling to cover another night. We called and learned there was a vacant room in Oceanside, so his points covered the additional night at no cost to us! We were so excited, and it was nice to rest another day after our long bike ride before heading back to reality at home.

During our bike ride back to Oceanside, we stopped off at a coffee shop so I could get a refreshing cup of iced coffee. Norm and I rested in some lounge chairs outside, and he mentioned that in addition to his usual leg pain, his stomach had begun to hurt him, as it had at times in the past. When we arrived back at the hotel, we showered and rested before dinner.

For our final night out, we planned on eating at the Crab Shack. On our walk to the restaurant, which was close to our hotel, we stopped and had someone take a photo of the two of us standing on the sand, with the ocean in the background. As we walked into the restaurant, Norm asked the hostess to take a photo of us with the boat scene in the bay behind us. I still have these special pictures, framed and hanging in my bedroom. They were taken on May 31, 2016, our anniversary.

The food was delicious, but Norm began to feel quite sick to his stomach and blamed it on the food he had ordered. He could not eat much, and we left soon after. He went to bed to rest as soon as we returned to our hotel. As everyone who knows me can guess, I was extremely worried about the changes I was seeing in Norm's physical health. At times I wondered why God works the way He does.

*The Lord will guide you always; he will satisfy your needs in a sun-scorched land and will strengthen your frame. You will be like a well-watered garden, like a spring whose waters never fail* (Isaiah 58:11).

When July came around, Brandon proposed to Brittany! They had been dating for about a year, and the previous month, Brandon had gone bowling with Norm to ask for his approval to marry Brittany. Norm had told him yes. Not long after that, Brandon planned to propose to Brittany. Family and friends knew about his plan, and I think Brittany figured it out as well.

After the proposal, Brandon's parents hosted a party at their house. While socializing at the get-together, Norm began swinging his left arm in a circle to help alleviate a painful flareup he was experiencing. I told him to please stop doing that. I was embarrassed and felt self-conscious of what others might think. As I am writing this account, and if you haven't come to realize it yet, I admit that I had a selfish, self-centered attitude at various times over the years.

*Do not let any unwholesome talk come out of your mouths, but only what is helpful for building others up according to their needs, that it may benefit those who listen* (Ephesians 4:29).

When August arrived, Norm and I held a large celebration to welcome Bryan home from Germany. The get-together also was an opportunity for everyone to see him before he left for Pennsylvania the following month. Bryan would be working on his PhD in comparative literature and teaching German.

Family members, close relatives, and friends came to congratulate and give Bryan their hugs good-bye. Later, my dad gave him a special toast, and Norm had his immediate family, which included Frank, Brandon, and Matt, join him on the grass area. Everyone then listened to Norm as he complimented us each individually on our accomplishments. He also shared meaningful, heartfelt thoughts about each of us, as we all toasted again with our beers.

September 12, 2016, is a day that I will never forget. Norm insisted that I take him to the ER at Placentia Linda Hospital. He was in terrible pain and could not bear it any longer. After a long wait, he was checked in, with his vitals taken, and settled into a room. He was given pain medication and IV fluids.

The next day, he would have an EGD done to examine the polyps on the walls of his stomach, with biopsies to determine a diagnosis of the pain he was experiencing. What followed was an eye-opening experience that I never thought I would have to process and digest.

When the EGD took place the following day, my mom came to the hospital to sit with me in the waiting room, along with my close friend Denise. After the procedure was done, I was called back into the recovery room to hear the results that the doctor had found. I stood closely beside Norm's bed.

Tears quickly began to roll down our faces, as the doctor proceeded to let us know that we would have to wait a few days to know for sure, but he was suspicious that Norm had cancer. Norm and I hugged, cried, and prayed together for a miracle. He remained in the hospital for a few more days, recovering until he had his strength back.

When I left the hospital later that evening, I remember pulling out of the parking lot and calling my dear friend, Lisa. I cried and cried and cried. I told her I would not be able to continue without Norm by my side. Lisa did not respond to me the way I was anticipating she would. I was expecting her words to be something like, "No, do not think that way… Norm will be okay." Instead, she loudly stated, "Yes, you can! You can make it on your own." She tried to calm me down and told me to wait until we found out more from the biopsies and not to make assumptions. My friend reminded me to continue praying for God's guidance.

I arrived home to tell Norm's dad and Brittany what the doctor had told us. Bryan had already left for Pennsylvania to begin school. That evening I had a difficult time sleeping and kept thinking about all the what ifs, without Norm lying next to me, close by my side. I had to return to work the following day, but I went to the hospital right after work and stayed with him until later in the evening.

On one of those days I was with him in the afternoon, a peculiar-looking man with crooked teeth approached Norm and introduced himself as the oncologist. What?! Why would the hospital send this type of doctor in to see Norm when we had not yet even heard the results from the doctor who did the procedure? Norm and I both felt a bit disturbed, unsettled, and to tell you the truth, shocked, but we did not talk about it as was our usual habit.

The few days that Norm was in the hospital went by slowly, and each time his gastroenterologist stopped in, Norm and I asked if there were any results yet from his EGD. No such luck. He was released and sent home to recover, continually taking norco for the pain, and he returned to work the next day.

That Friday, September 16, either one or two days after his release from the hospital, Norm phoned me right after I got off work. I answered, as I was sitting in my car in the parking lot, and he said, "Hey, good lookin', what's cookin'?" I responded hello, and then he began to tell me the news that he had just been told by his doctor on a phone call. As he began crying, Norm said, "I have stage 4 cancer!"

I did not know what to do or whom to turn to, so I drove to see Mom. She opened the front door, and I burst into tears, while telling her our life-changing news. My mom grabbed me, wrapping her arms around me, holding me quite tightly. She then began to say that the doctors would take care of Norm and told me that everything would be alright.

My nephew Chris was also over at their house, and he had heard my words from the kitchen. He came to the front door, hugged me, and told me how deeply sorry he was. My mom invited me inside, but I told her I needed to leave soon so I could be there before Norm arrived home. At this point in my life, it seemed there was no answer to my question, "Why, God, do You put trials and tribulations in my life, and how can these moments bring me closer to You?"

Why should I keep writing? Perhaps I should start another book, hoping to find a future answer to this intense, complicated question. My faith and hope are important to share, as I continue to write here about more challenges through these trials with Norm's health issues, and how God walked with me, step by step, every inch of the way.

# ⌢22⌢

## Is This It?

Norm arrived home, and our minds both wondered as we began to seek further so-called answers to our many prayers. We both held each other closely and cried along with Brittany and Norm Sr. The doctor had told Norm that it was stage 4 cancer in his stomach, and he would need to have his liver looked at also, as it looked suspicious. He was to begin his chemotherapy and radiation ASAP.

Most of September was a blur for us. We felt overwhelmed while life went on for everyone else. We celebrated my parents fifty-sixth wedding anniversary with Sherrie and Pat at the Elks Club. We all sat as I tried to enjoy dinner, but Norm could not get comfortable in his chair, and he did not eat much.

I know you are probably expecting to see a verse now that explains or helps us to understand more clearly and relate to this situation better but, no… I just cannot think of one. Norm had very reluctantly scheduled an appointment with the oncologist to get started fighting the cancer. Unfortunately, he was scheduled with the same man whom we had seen previously at Placentia Linda Hospital, during his time as a patient.

As Norm and I sat in the waiting room, we were surrounded by other very quiet, subdued patients, with and without hair. I was wondering what must have been going through Norm's mind at this time in his life. We finally were called in, and as we spoke with the oncologist, he wanted to immediately begin the chemotherapy so it would reduce the cancer found in his stomach.

Norm then asked about the inconclusive findings in his liver. The doctor told us that we should first begin the chemotherapy on his stomach for now. After leaving the office, Norm loudly insisted on getting a second opinion, declaring that he refused to be seen by this doctor again.

Norm had occasionally been feeling colder in our house for quite some time before the diagnosis. He was more tired at night and had less energy during the day, as I had noticed in Germany. Norm had also lost twenty pounds, chalking it up to attempting to eat less to lose a few. I had ignored little clues like these that pointed to something more serious, not wanting to face the possibility that his health condition might have progressed to cancer, which is such a scary word.

Toward the end of September, Norm was again in excruciating pain, and my dad came with me to take him to the ER at UCI Medical Center. Because it was known as a research hospital, this was where Norm wanted to go. There were multiple doctors there in each field, collaborating on research and advanced healthcare and treatment. Hopefully we could receive different advice on treatment that could provide a more positive, definitive path.

We had brought down a wheelchair from the ER to push Norm up to the overly crowded waiting room. After waiting over two hours, they finally checked him in, connected him to an IV, and then proceeded to perform a CT scan of his liver. I sat next to Norm's bed in a dark, small corner room. He began feeling a bit better while we waited because they had increased his Norco pain medication. Norm dozed off, and we ended up staying overnight waiting for the tests results.

The following morning, I specifically remember the doctor strolling in, along with resident doctors. Unfortunately, we were given the news that the cancer had also spread to his liver. His lungs looked questionable as well. At this stage of the disease, the doctors reaffirmed our decision to get a second opinion at their hospital, because treatment and medication for the cancer would be different, depending on where all the cancer was found.

As we left for home that day, Norm planned on proceeding with chemotherapy, although he was really dreading it. He was very tired, and since we had first received the diagnosis in the middle of September, he had not returned to work. His energy was very low, and the pain was quite intense. So much sad news had happened in such a short period of time. The following week, our Care Group Bible study was held at our home. Norm was in too much pain to leave the house.

On the evening of Friday, October 9, Norm again was experiencing extreme pain, and I literally forced him in the car and drove to UCI ER. He did not want to go in the first place, because he could not stand the thought of waiting two to three hours in pain, in the waiting room, to be seen again. I am sure I was not the only family member in the ER waiting room who insisted their loved one be seen right away! After a long wait, Norm was attached to an IV for pain relief, then eventually admitted into the hospital.

Those next ten days were the hardest, most painful, and depressing days I had faced in my life. I was buried in grief, while trying to stay informed and remember all the information and treatment we were faced with. I was fifty-two years old and had spent thirty-one of those years with Norm, my best friend.

Norm called Bryan in Pennsylvania and told him that he was in the hospital now with stage 4 cancer in his stomach and liver. Norm had not wanted to bother him since he had just left for UPENN, at least not until we knew more in detail. A few days later, Bryan had booked a flight to come home from his first month of college away.

I slept on a fold-out bed each night, right beside his bed, because I did not want him to face this journey alone. After he was admitted, crowds of friends and family came to visit, filling up the waiting room on weekends. It was a comfort and especially helpful to me. I was not alone, and I continually had loved ones who sat next to my side.

I remember on Monday, a short man walked into Norm's room. He was the chaplain of the hospital, and Norm was happy to meet with him. It was typical of Norm to greet all doctors, nurses, and any other hospital personnel with a smile, asking them if he could pray for them, regardless of the pain he was in. He did the same with the chaplain. This man was shocked and amazed at Norm's offer and smiled, replying to Norm that he was supposed to be the one praying for him!

The main doctor in charge, along with the resident doctors, reviewed Norm's medical notes and checked on him daily. His doctor continually commented each visit, for three to four days in a row, that Norm would most likely be released the following day. I was eagerly staying busy, following up with trying to make appointments for Norm to begin his "non-engaging" treatments of chemotherapy once he was released. I was impatient and afraid to lose any time in this race against cancer!

I remember on Tuesday, Norm experienced intense pain, and we were both awake around 2 a.m. He sat uncomfortably in a chair across from the bed while I sat next to him. We were both in tears. It was heartbreaking for me to see him in so much pain, and I told him, "We can get through this together!"

Norm then changed his focus from the pain and discussed coming up with a "bucket list" for both of us to enjoy once he had recovered. He quickly started the list with a trip to Alaska, where he would teach me how to fish. He had been thinking about this quite a bit. We then had our bucket list started with a trip planned for our thirty-first anniversary the following May.

As you might have noticed, since this all began with three

different visits to the ER within the last month, I had not found a Bible verse that might correlate with the situation going on at that time. It is difficult, even now, almost four years later, to write and revisit all that happened at this time in my life.

Yes, I began this book a little over a year ago, as it had been three years since this trial had entered our everyday lives. Looking back and reflecting, I now believe that sometimes life can seem so awful, but God is still there, even when I am at my weakest spiritually and cannot draw on a specific Bible verse to guide my path. The following verse is one that I can relate to today in a different frame of mind, with a stronger faith that sustained me the last few years:

*The Lord himself goes before you and will be with you; he will never leave you nor forsake you. Do not be afraid; do not be discouraged* (Deuteronomy 31:8).

Obviously, during that period, I was barely keeping track of my thinking, energy, and daily devotions; I was spread thin mentally and physically. One person who was by my side every day was Debbie, our close friend for many years. She was there to take thorough notes in a wide, blue notebook for me, when different doctors would come in or when testing would take place. My mother was there almost every day; Sherrie was there on her days off work. Also, my dear friend Lisa was often visiting, along with relatives and many close friends.

On Wednesday, the doctors performed an ultrasound to look at his stomach again and saw the cancer was also in his lungs, as predicted before. The cancer was rapidly spreading, first in his stomach, then in his liver, and now in his lungs.

Bryan arrived at the hospital from Pennsylvania, and Sarah also came home from school in Flagstaff to be by their dad's side. When Thursday came along, we were told for the last time that Norm would be feeling better and well enough to go home on

Friday, the next day.

Norm's energy was decreasing, so he started to talk and visit less, because he wanted to sleep more and be left alone. His drowsiness increased due to the dosage of the morphine needed to manage his pain. He specifically wanted to speak with my dad by himself, with regard to our finances for the future.

I remember talking with our niece Audry, who was there next to her Uncle Norm in the hospital. We spoke about her grandpa, Norm's dad. At this time, I specifically felt that Norm's dad needed to move out and find another place to live, rather than stay in our home. I felt that when Norm was able to go home, there was going to be a lot of tension while he went through chemotherapy and radiation. It would be very difficult for me to help Norm with his health issues, as well as be responsible for Norm Sr. Audry fully understood and began to look for a place for her grandpa to move.

Friday came. It had been eight days since Norm was admitted to UCI Medical Center. The day before, his body began to swell up, especially his arms and legs. The nurses and doctors informed us that it probably was due to him not being up and moving around.

Even though Norm was quite tired from the morphine, during the week, he was determined and had tried a few times to walk in a circle down the hall. I was walking alongside him, helping with all his IV contraptions as Norm took a break, resting on the bench in the waiting room. Before heading back to his room, the last time on our journey down the hall, Norm seemed very disturbed about the future.

# ⁓23⁓

# The Big Light of Mine

Later in the day on Friday, Norm was rolled downstairs in his hospital bed for a total body PET scan. I believe the doctor was now questioning why Norm was still there and had not progressed enough to be released "the following day," as we had continually been told would happen. We looked into each other's eyes, both of us in tears. I grabbed his hand and pulled it toward me. I told him, "We can do this. You are going to be okay! I love you."

When they brought Norm back to the room, I was by myself. After the doctor returned with Norm, he bluntly proceeded to tell us that the tests showed the cancer had spread throughout his body and that Norm was not going to make it for much longer. Yes, he said this with me sitting there!

I tried to swallow this news, which was so incredibly difficult to digest. The doctor gave us this information very bluntly, which came off as abrasive and without concern, at least to me. When I heard these words, I grabbed my phone at my side to text Lisa... "I need you now!"

The doctor did not seem as concerned as he had been throughout the past week for Norm. I am not sure if down deep inside, he had begun to really like Norm, and now he felt guilty for saying over and over to us that his patient was in the process of recovery and soon to be released. Maybe Norm had planted a seed in his beliefs.

Norm did not have a lot of energy, so he did not have much

to say. The doctor then rudely asked, "How do you want to be buried?" There was none of the compassion so desperately needed in this situation. Norm quickly replied that he wanted to be buried in the ground. I then spoke to Norm and said, "Why don't we just do ashes because of affordability? It won't matter because your soul is going straight to heaven."

He agreed as he closed his eyes again, and I sat there, thinking that this certainly would be a time I will never forget. After the doctor left, Norm then said, "I wish I would have known this was going to happen, so that I could have brought him closer to knowing Jesus." The doctor had told us recently that he was Buddhist. Norm was still concerned about another person's faith, knowing he would not be with us much longer!

Lisa arrived soon after, followed by family and friends. I am not quite sure of specific details, or maybe I have much of it blocked out of my head, as there were many different ideas, thoughts, emotions, and opinions going on at this time. So much took place soon after, with many other people coming in to say their last good-byes to Norm.

All my kids had made the choice and asked me if we could keep Dad in the hospital as they were afraid that he would die in the ambulance, away from them, while he traveled back home. I agreed, and our precious kids also made the decision, in the hospital, to take his ashes to Alaska the following summer, as that is where their dad wanted to go next, the first item on our bucket list. We would go as a family and pour his ashes in the water where Norm had wanted to teach me how to fish.

Norm had asked for a pastor from our church to come in and pray over him. The pastor came to the hospital in the evening, and as Norm sat in his cushioned chair, he said a prayer and blessed him with oil, as many others prayed over him. We both said to one another, "I love you."

Frank slept in a chair in the room that night. He helped me

feed Norm and took him to the restroom the next day. I was emotional and still in shock because this had happened so fast, having recently come screaming into our lives.

On Saturday, Norm's eyes were closed much of the day. He became less responsive each day from Friday to Sunday, and I did not leave his side. I sat beside Norm, glued to him on the bed all day, and sleeping on the rollout bed for a few hours at night.

Brandon and Brittany, who were planning to be married in January the following year, asked their pastor to marry them there in the hospital room. Norm was given the opportunity to perform his role as the "father of the bride" and answer "I do," to the traditional question, releasing his daughter to the groom in marriage. This was a tearful wedding, without much joy, as Brittany would not have her dad to walk next to her down the aisle.

People took turns coming in to see Norm, and his dad, Norm Sr., came to say his last good-bye. Audry was visiting a lot, staying by my side. She had experienced this painful situation with her mom and grandma. Later in the evening, Frank and Nichole had said they were coming to say good-bye, it seemed, holding back tears, as they had made previous plans to fly the next day to Hawaii. Bryan was going to stay in the room with me that evening and sleep in a chair.

On Sunday, October 18, Norm did not function well; he simply lay with his eyes closed all day in bed. He was not eating anymore and just breathing now with the help of a machine. About midday, Norm was on his side in bed, and I wanted to lie next to him again. I asked the nurse if she could scoot him to the middle and another nurse came in to help lift him together and repositioned him.

Norm then suddenly jolted after he was moved, and a terrified feeling went through my mind: "Is this it?" No, he was still okay, and I rested next to him in bed. We all knew the time was getting closer.

My parents, my sister, and our relatives all gave their farewells to Norm. Bryan, Brittany, and Sarah, along with Brandon and Matt, came in that evening and kissed their dad and future father-in-law good-bye. It just did not seem real to me that our time was finally coming to an end. It was a surreal feeling, like a story you read or a movie you watch that is so great that you do not want it to end.

Two especially important couples we had known through church for a long time, Jay and Jana and Greg and Janet, were at the hospital toward the end. Lisa stayed with me by my side, as I needed her more than I ever could have imagined. As everyone left, Lisa and my brother Donald were in the waiting room, and Greg and Janet were the last ones in with Norm and me. They added one last thing that touched me deep inside. They told me that Norm was now waiting for me to say good-bye. They both said good-bye to Norm and left the room.

After a few minutes, when he moved again quickly, I looked at Norm's face and took a deep breath, then said, "I will be okay, Norm. You can go. I will be strong and have faith."

Immediately, he lifted his head off the pillow, which he had not done for two days, opened his eyes wide, and looked me straight in my eyes as I lay beside him. I thought for just a moment that he was being healed and was going to be okay!

At around 9:00 on Sunday, October 18, he rested back his head quickly, closed his eyes, and his soul was raised up to heaven! I screamed, cried, and sang at my loudest, "This little light of mine, I'm going to let it shine, this little light of mine, I'm going to let it shine, let it shine, let it shine, let it shine. Don't let Satan blow it out, I'm going to let it shine…" and I continued crying and singing throughout the song.

Donald came into the room, and I told him to read Norm's favorite Bible verse, Philemon 1:6:

*I pray that your partnership with us in the faith may be ef-*

*fective in deepening your understanding of every good thing we share for the sake of Christ* (Philemon 1:6).

Lisa came in, and we wept and wept and wept, with her holding me tightly and Donald grabbing onto me at the same time. We packed up my belongings, and Lisa took me home, where my kids greeted me at the front door, wrapping their arms around me as I walked in, unable to stop the tears from flowing. The next day would have been thirty-one years since Norm and I became engaged on October 19, 1985.

When Nichole and Frank returned from Hawaii the following weekend, they came over and spent time with me along with my other kids. I remember clearly, as I was crying in the shower, my daughters emptying out all of Norm's clothing in the drawers and off the hangers in the closet, along with his shoes. They then put his belongings in boxes and placed them out in the garage. They thought by taking all his clothing out of sight, it would be less of a reminder to me of their dad. Nichole did keep several of his shirts, my favorite, hanging in the closet, as I had asked. This was much too soon to do such a large change at the undetachable stage of grief that I had just started.

I can honestly say that during the next year ahead, I do not remember a whole lot that took place, as my memory was again in a very disturbed and unpleasant blur. Surely I was covered with warm hearts during this cold, empty time of life. I still felt deep down that I was alone and on my own in so many challenging ways.

Many close friends and family brought me meals, flowers, gifts, hugs, prayers, comforting talks, and simple company when I needed it most. Denise and Madalyn began joining me on my daily walks each morning with Harper. Mom, Dad, Sherrie, and Lisa were with me, sharing their loving smiles and stretched out arms of comfort. My financial future was guided by my father, with the help of Lisa.

Debbie, who was by my side so often at the hospital, took over the job of making the plans for a Celebration of Life, honoring Norm's passing. She was able to book a date in November at Friends Community Church, and Pastor Jim would be able to conduct the ceremony. Norm had enjoyed listening to Jim speak in the past at RDFC, and he said he would be honored to lead the service. I asked if his wife could sing, as I remember I adored her voice in the choir.

A few weeks or so after Norm passed away, I returned to work. While dealing with my grief and facing my life-changing battle, I was transferred to Tyne's Elementary School. I had applied to a position shortly before Norm's quick decline. I was still going to be working with autistic preschool-age children. I thought I would be able to adjust to the new surroundings, but my heart was not in it, and I had a difficult time avoiding tears… I lasted a week, but with advice and support from loved ones, I finally accepted that I needed to take time off to cope with my grief and new life.

Preparing for the funeral, memorial, or what is nowadays called a celebration, was not an easy time to experience. Looking through pictures of our family adventures and traditions was extremely painful. Sherrie helped me scan photos that were chosen from all my many albums that Nichole, Brittany, Sarah, and I had looked through to make a video to share. Bryan had returned to college in Pennsylvania a short time after Norm's passing.

I had put together a frame full of memorable photos of our recent trip to Encinitas and Oceanside for our thirtieth anniversary. This collage, along with many other keepsakes, including a photo album of the many trips we took together, were going to be displayed on a few tables as my special memories of my lifetime with Norm.

November came, and the date was set for November 12, 2016. It still makes me sad to this day, just to remember looking at that enlarged picture of Norm placed on a stand at the church altar, looking at me but knowing that he was not coming home. The service was so very long and difficult to make it through, holding together in one piece, as my tears fell to the floor.

I remember Bryan sitting on one side of me and Sarah on the other, holding me close to their hearts, with their arms glued to me the entire time. It was a packed church, about three hundred people, and Bryan stood up and shared at the altar special memories he had with his dad.

As we walked outside when the service was over, others formed a line to come give me their condolences. To my surprise, I was able to make it through that seemingly long process, one of many more difficult things to go through.

The kids all took me down to the beach, and we went out to dinner, sharing at a circular table our most important thoughts of happiness, trying to keep back tears for a short time, of their dad. He was my husband, my closest friend, faith leader, teacher, helper, love of my life, here on earth and in heaven, forevermore.

It was over now, and reality without Norm set in for me. I wanted to give up, and I wondered if there was really a person called God who would allow this to happen. I had told Norm many times in the past that I wanted to be the first one to die, not him. I had said it jokingly, but deep down I did not want him to leave me behind, stranded without his care, love, and the wholesomeness I so desperately wanted, needed, and adored. I remember sitting on my couch one day alone and screaming at the top of my voice. It did not help; life had not miraculously changed, and Norm was still gone.

Bryan went back to UPenn again and planned to return for Christmas. My close friends, Madalyn, Debbie, and Ronda, as well as my sister Sherrie, at different times, held me together with their loving arms and encouragement at church. I began attending Friends Community Church in December. I felt this was now my home church.

Days went slow, and weeks went even slower, as each morning I would wake up and roll over, thinking I would see Norm next to me in bed. I tried my hardest to help Brittany and Brandon with their wedding preparations for the following year in January, but with an insincere smile on my face. I could only do so much, as this was not at all what I wanted to take part in at this time. I had no energy, and I felt like I was living in a cloud.

Soon I was faced with a leak in my house during the month of December. I had no strength or wisdom to deal with it. The leak was coming from the garage, into two of the interior rooms. Fortunately, my father took charge. After a few long months, this was taken care of, and two rooms were repaired with new dry-wall, paint, and who knows what else, along with carpet too.

During the large flood process, repairs, and painting, Christmas came. I had no feelings to even put into perspective a celebration of Christmas without Norm. My kids certainly made this a season I would never forget.

They had planned beforehand, with a grocery shopping list, to continue with Dad's past tradition of making a huge breakfast on Christmas morning. This was always done after the gifts were finished being unwrapped. Brandon and Brittany had to leave soon after the gifts were opened, and they chose not to be a part of that Christmas tradition.

As we sat down at the table for the homemade breakfast of hash browns, eggs, bacon, and pancakes with chocolate chips, each family member shared something they were thankful for about their dad and my husband.

Another important part of that first Christmas without Norm, after the breakfast, we came up with a saying to put on a block to be made for their dad. Huntsman Cancer Research had told us they were making a block for memories of Norm to display next to the hospital in Utah.

There were so many donations given in remembrance of

Norm, at the celebration, that would pay for the block, and around the breakfast table we brainstormed and finalized what would be engraved on the block. It read:

Fisher of Men
Norman N. Norton, 1961–2016
Philemon 1:6.

I hope someday to have the opportunity to travel to Utah and view this special block with my husband's name on it.

# ☙24☙

# Footsteps Leading

January 2017 was the beginning of another new chapter in my life. I was living on my own without Norm, and Brittany and Brandon were married on the twenty-first. Lisa was there for me, and I would not have been able to make it through the wedding without her. She is such a dear friend, who again was by my side, supporting me on a very special day for Brittany.

Anton came to join us from Germany, as did Bryan from Pennsylvania, and they helped me as well, along with Nichole, Frank, Matt, and Sarah, to make it through another turning point in my life. I do not remember many details from this special day, other than missing Norm, whom I wished so badly could have walked Brittany down the church aisle. I walked side by side, arm in arm with her, as I cried. This was more difficult than any words could explain, but it was just the beginning of many days, weeks, months, and years to come.

Bryan flew back to UPenn, Brittany was off living her new married life, and I was home alone in my small house, which now felt exceptionally large to me by myself. I had a long year ahead of me. A friend from church made me a precious blanket with all of Norm's meaningful shirts that I had kept. I held it each night and thought of Norm, who could not be by my side.

One day at the beginning of 2017, I came home and found a note on the kitchen table from Brittany. She must have come by the house while I was at work, and it read as follows:

Hi Mom,

I was here for lunch lol.

I thought I would leave a Bible verse/passage with you today. I hope it gives you strength.

Psalm 23:1-4

*The Lord is my shepherd; I shall not want. He makes me lie down in green pastures. He leads me beside still waters. He restores my soul. He leads me in paths of righteousness for his name's sake. Even though I walk through the valley of the shadow of death, I will fear no evil; for you are with me; your rod and your staff, they comfort me.*

Love, your daughter,

Brittany

God continued to secure me in times of need. I had my second leak since Norm had passed, and the shower in my bathroom was needing to be replaced, due to the leak. Parents and friends helped me with their input, ideas, and assistance in choosing replacements for the shower and the sink, along with touchups here and there.

Of course, it was another major expense, and my dad helped again with the financial details. My dad, Lisa, and my kids were a huge part of helping with financial decisions regarding such things. God blessed me with family and friends supporting me and surrounding me with their love. These were stressful times for me, and it felt as if I was pulling a heavy wheelbarrow several miles during my many trials.

In April, I wanted to spend Easter with Bryan in Philadelphia. His birthday was also coming up, so it was a good time to visit. My parents decided to join me and stay in a hotel while I stayed with Bryan and his girlfriend. Dad and Mom were concerned about me traveling alone, and I was happy they joined me for the trip. We stayed busy, touring around the city, and taking a walk on the UPenn campus. We also took a drive to Washington, DC, and saw many sights in the rain.

In May, Brittany finished her fifth year at Cal State Fullerton. After her graduation ceremony, we celebrated at my house with family and friends. It certainly was difficult getting through this celebration without Norm sitting next to me and cheering Brittany on, as he had done at so many of her soccer games.

It was also hard for me to think of our house as "mine," rather than "ours." It is still difficult to do, as I write about these memories. May 31 would have been our thirty-first wedding anniversary, so family and friends took me to dinner and comforted me, as this was hard to celebrate now as a widow.

August arrived, and Frank, Nichole, Bryan, Matt, Sarah, and I flew to Alaska. This was the trip they had planned when their dad was dying, almost a year before. This trip was not a happy, meaningful, beautiful, memorable, or pleasant vacation. I do not want to go into detail about it.

In many ways, it brought so many heartbreaking, frustrating, and depressing thoughts to my mind, as I saw many ports on the waterfront, among other things, that reminded me of Norm. Brandon and Brittany had decided not to go with us.

I do remember, though, the difficult but meaningful day when we all went out on a boat. We were in the middle of the deep blue sea, off the shore of Alaska. We each tearfully shared deep thoughts and feelings about Norm as we individually tossed his ashes into the sea. He did not get to teach me how to fish there, but this moment was very peaceful.

Soon after, in September, Brandon and Brittany were moving to England. Brandon was going to continue working on his PhD, which would allow him to become a professor teaching the Old Testament. This was another personal milestone I would have to get through on my own. It was hard to have another one of my kids move so far away.

Within this time frame, I began to attend a Grief Recovery Group that was offered through my church. The therapist who led the class is quite a special lady. When the class began, I was very depressed and emotional, but Sherrie came with me several times, encouraging me and helping me, with her arms wrapped around me. The class was extremely helpful and uplifting. I slowly progressed in baby steps, strengthening my understanding and acceptance of Norm being gone.

I did not feel as consumed by the Bible until almost a year after Norm passed. When I slowly began to understand more, through the recovery group, I was seeing the beginning of where God was directing my path, and how I would slowly be leaning on His Word more often.

*He reached down from on high and took hold of me; he drew me out of deep waters. He rescued me from my powerful enemy, from my foes, who were too strong for me. They confronted me in the day of my disaster, but the Lord was my support. He brought me out into a spacious place; he rescued me because he delighted in me* (Psalm 18:16–19).

October 18 quickly arrived—a year to the day since Norm had died. It flew by in some ways, but it dragged slowly in others. With many trials and tribulations, which included Brittany getting married and moving far away, home repairs, financial decisions, everyday decisions on my own, I cried with fear without my second half, yet I had made it through this year, having my faith pull me by His side.

# ~25~

# Trials in Therapy

In August 2017, my Aunt Carolyn passed away from a brain aneurism, and on October 24, Sherrie's husband, Pat, had a sudden heart attack and passed away. Within one year's timespan, there had been many deaths in our family. It was a year I would not want to repeat.

Thanksgiving was approaching. Matt and Sarah had invited my parents and me to celebrate the holiday with them. I stayed in their apartment, while my folks rented a hotel close by. This certainly was a hard time to acknowledge what I truly was thankful for. As we sat at the table with our turkey dinner, we went around taking turns expressing our gratefulness, a familiar tradition of Norm's in the past.

December approached, and Sarah had scheduled to have her colon removed to beat the ongoing polyps from increasing and turning to cancer. The procedure went well, and she was home at my house for her Christmas break from school, since this was a good time to undergo this major procedure and long recovery. Matt was by her side throughout the entire recovery and still is joyfully today.

At the beginning of January 2018, I began seeing a professional therapist I had met through Grief Recovery. I went to counseling each week until the end of May. She helped me so much at this time when I needed personal therapy desperately. She helped me get through the trials that God had placed in my life.

My therapist was also a special blessing with our one-on-one conversations, teaching, laughter, and tears. I knew God had placed her in my life. I began to be interested in reading and learning on my own, as she recommended the book, *The Gifts of Imperfection*, by Brené Brown. This book helped me to slowly and gradually build up my self-confidence and self-esteem.

During January, my parents were in the process of moving into a senior living facility. I continued to help in the process of gathering belongings stored for many of my growing-up years in their home. They planned to sell our family home, filled with memories, in the future. We had slowly been working on going through personal odds and ends, trying to get rid of accumulated stuff, but packing in many boxes most of the treasures to move with them.

In February, Nichole had scheduled to have her colon removed, for the same reason as Sarah had done so in December. She and Frank kept it to themselves until the procedure was over, and she then came out to tell me what she had done, while I was visiting at their home. I was happy she was strong enough to have the procedure done and be proactive regarding her health.

My parents had been in the senior living facility for a few months, and we still were unloading and clearing out accumulations at their previous home, which they were close to listing for sale. They then decided to rent a four-bedroom home around the corner from their original house, and slowly move back all of their belongings.

We had moved them once, and now were going to do it again—packing, unpacking, packing, and moving again. They moved in May to the rented house and sold their home around the block not long after that. I never enjoyed the whole process of moving, but this really "frosted the cake," so to speak.

At the end of May, my mom and dad, Nichole, Frank, Matt's parents, and I took part in a happy celebration for Sarah's college graduation from NAU in Arizona. We had an enjoyable time visiting and then moving her back to my house, as she had many preparations for her wedding to Matt in August.

I remember in the hospital, when Norm was unable to speak anymore, Matt had asked his permission to marry Sarah, without getting a response back. Matt was sad that he had not done this beforehand, but he felt that Norm's blessings had been sent his way, through his future mother-in-law's good wishes for the two of them.

I also finished my therapy in May. I had made a strong and secure process of beginning to build my confidence and gradually working on becoming more of an independent person, welcoming my need to continue growing for my future. I continued a new habit of reading, as my therapist had suggested a few books that have helped me a lot.

The first was on building my self-confidence and facing what was in the future, with the book I mentioned previously. I hurried through that one, outlining and folding many pages, before starting the next book, *Boundaries*, by Cloud and Townsend. These also were helpful and encouraged me in my independent growth process.

Through this personal therapy time, along with the time devoted to the Grief Support Group and the books I read, I realized and accepted something about myself. I could have, in the past, worked on being a humble, more supportive, and caring wife at times. I was persistent in getting my way quite often during our marriage, and I did not take into consideration Norm's feelings, opinions, or decisions.

This shortcoming of mine is most likely apparent to anyone reading my book, which shares so much of our thirty years of marriage. Remembering and writing about my journey has been important for me to share, and it has been a very meaningful part of my growth process. I am hoping and praying this book is meaningful to you in some way also.

*I have told you these things, so that in me you may have peace. In this world you will have trouble. But take heart! I have overcome the world* (John 16:33).

# ≈26≈

## Cross Made with Beads

In July, it was time for Matt and Sarah to move their belongings to their new apartment in Phoenix, where they would move the following month after their wedding. I joined Matt's parents in helping with my good ol' truck. During this busy weekend of moving, I began thinking of beginning my own business.

I had previously relearned how to make macramé plant holders in 2016. I thought perhaps I could pick up my old hobby and use these as gifts for many helpful hearts. It kept me busy and helped take my mind off sadness, and that gave me more focus on what I could do with my life ahead.

I was excited and spoke with Matt and Sarah about my new hobby, which I had learned long ago in seventh-grade art class. They both encouraged me, so I began with intense plans when I arrived home to begin my own business. So many ideas scrambled in my head, as this, I am certain, was another plan God had on His agenda to keep my mind off the depressing, sorrowful thoughts of my past. My business took on the name: "Good Lookin' Décor."

I was excited to do this on my own, enjoying what I did, and my new business had a very meaningful name. Norm, if you recall, would often say to me, "Hey, good lookin', what's cookin'?" So, I narrowed the title down, and this became my new logo, and on each piece of décor, I used beads within the macramé to enhance the items, adding a section with beads in the shape of a small cross. This, to me, was a special symbol of Norm as being part of my macramé artwork, and I prayed for each person who purchased them, hoping that they would come to know or deepen their relationship with God.

During the summer, I also made the choice to sell our ski and fishing boat, which had been sitting unused at the side of the house for at least five years. This "dream come true" addition to our family had brought so many enjoyable, memorable, strenuous at times, moments I would never forget.

A couple from church volunteered to come over, and we washed the boat and made a few minor repairs, and then he put it on Craig's List to sell it. Not long after, a man came to look at it. He and his son were interested in purchasing the boat for $3,100.

The man's son came over to pick up the boat with his truck. Signing the pink slip with Norm's name was quite difficult to do, yet with a few tears and a message to the guy picking it up, my heart was at peace with this big decision. I told him I would pray that he and his family would enjoy the boat as much as my family had throughout the years.

August 4, 2018 was quite a special day, especially for Matt and Sarah, as this was their wedding day. Before the ceremony at Oak Canyon Nature Center, the group of ladies in her wedding party and I stood in a circle, with arms around one another, and we prayed for the remarkable day and their life ahead. That was such a meaningful moment to share with one another, sharing our thoughts with Sarah on her blessed day. I stood among the bridal party with my arms gathered around my daughters.

Labor Day weekend came next, and I drove with my parents in their old, spacious van to carry Matt and Sarah's remaining gifts from their wedding to Arizona. By that time, I had begun to measure and cut the amounts of cotton rope needed for my macramé artwork, which I had excitedly ordered. I was ready to begin my independent hobby.

On the long road trip in the back seat of the van, I began my to-do list as well as measuring and cutting away to make several different plant holders and wall hangings. In Arizona, Dad and Matt both helped me design a business card and a flyer/handout with my logo on it, with a cross in the background. It read:

# Good Lookin' Décor
## *Macramé Artwork by Suzy*
- Wall Hangings
- Plant Holders
- Key Chains

I earnestly began planning events to show off and sell my new products. I was having an enjoyable time making decorations with meaningful blessings inspired by Norm tied into the artwork. I worked on my first plant holder creation while visiting Matt and Sarah.

During the month of September, I was faced with selling my favorite Ford truck. It had served our family well: carpooling, taking us on fun family excursions, vacations towing our boat, soccer games, weekend getaways, and other countless adventures. I went to get it checked out and learned that it needed a new engine.

It was going to cost too much, and the truck was incredibly old, but I still loved it! I felt safe and tall when I drove it, as the truck sat up high off the ground. I went out with Nichole on a car hunt to find a replacement. Both these situations were more steps I needed to take in pursuing my independence.

Nichole and I headed to CarMax. She encouraged me and brought a smile to my face in making yet another change in my life ahead. We began the negotiations, then a problem arose. Another person wanted the same car we had chosen, and we had both taken it for a trial run around the block.

Nichole and I were patiently waiting, sitting next to each

other, for the two sellers to come to an agreement on who had the priority in purchasing this special car. Nichole then took my hand and said, "Let's pray about it," and she did so with confidence and faith that God would provide, whether it was with this car or with another one.

Soon after the prayer ended, our salesman came out and handed me the keys to my new car! We were both so thankful for God's direction, and we began the long process with much paperwork for me to fill out and sign, with Nichole by my side. Eventually, after some time, my last signature was made as an individual owner of a new car.

This, of course, brought happy, yet sad tears, as I missed Norm being there in charge, making the final signatures, on a very large financial decision. I walked outside to see my sharp, clean, dark blue 2012 Honda CRV. It had a huge bow tied around it, and I proudly stood next to it with a confident smile.

October arrived, and a special weekend approached to help me walk through the second year from when Norm went to heaven. Lisa invited me on a four-day cruise to Catalina Island and Ensenada. I had never been on a cruise before, and I was excited to spend this adventure with her. We had a special time with each other buried in our close friendship together.

While stopping off in Catalina, we rented electric bikes and rode them on a trail up to the top of the mountain, being tourists with the decorative scenery, looking down on the crowded, main city of Avalon. After our viewing excursion on the bike ride, we relaxed and sat at a restaurant along the boardwalk, looking out onto the ocean, eating one of our favorites, chips and salsa, along with sharing a Corona light beer.

We then ventured on the cruise to Ensenada, where we quickly walked off board to a few shops and then back onto the ship to relax, read, sunbathe, and enjoy each other in conversation. The time together was meaningful in my continued healing and led me closer in wanting to find someone else to fill that other half of my heart in a relationship.

In the remaining months of 2018, I continued to be busy with my macramé artwork. Designing away, I displayed and sold them at Christmas boutiques during November and December. I also sold several of my Good Lookin' Décor macramé to friends, family, and at work, where I had them on display. What made me even more pleased and proud of my sales was that I gave a percentage of each sale to the Huntsman Cancer Institute, where Norm had been seen in Utah.

# ≈27≈

# On the Lookout

Growing in all these steps of my journey of independence, I began thinking it might be time to find a companion with whom I could share life. In November, two years after Norm died, I decided to take off my wedding ring. This was, for certain, not an easy transition to make.

My goal now was to try out new churches, to find someone to meet in a larger group of believers. I thought certainly, if I began attending a larger church worshiping God, He would find me a special person to meet and begin a relationship with! I then began church hopping and on the lookout.

*Meanwhile, the moment we get tired in the waiting, God's Spirit is right alongside helping us along. If we don't know how or what to pray, it doesn't matter. He does our praying in and for us, making prayer out of our wordless sighs, our aching groans. He knows us far better than we know ourselves, knows our pregnant condition, and keeps us present before God. That's why we can be so sure that every detail in our lives of love for God is worked into something good* (Romans 8:26–28 MSG).

The year 2019 began, and I decided to check out EV Free Church in January, as I had previously been told that they had a singles Sunday school group. Maybe I could meet the man of my dreams there. I enjoyed the service, the atmosphere, the friendly people, and the singles Sunday school class each week.

I found out, through the Sunday school class, about a new book to read, *Safe People*, again by Cloud and Townsend, the same authors of the previous book I had read. I thoroughly enjoyed reading, highlighting, and folding pages over to remind me and to guide me for my life ahead as a widow. I remember a meaningful quote from this book, which read, "Gain wisdom and discernment through knowledge and experience."

I certainly have put this message into good use again and again through my future dating and in relationships with friends and family. After attending EV Free for about five months, I decided to go back to Rose Drive Friends Church and give it another try. I was finding that the church I had been attending since January was not where I was fitting in.

With my new side career, macramé artwork, I began selling several pieces at my mom's beauty salon nearby, where I could display various items. I sold key chains, wall hangings, and plant holders. I also took personal orders for custom pieces. In addition, I began displaying and selling my artwork at my own hairdresser's salon, along with a flower store across the street.

Close to Mother's Day in May, I sold many plant holders with the store's plants in them, hanging on display, so we both made a profit, which was great. I had these displays on site for a few months at each location, and it kept me busy at home with my mind occupied, in a positive, fulfilling way. When I finished using the last spool of rope I had ordered, I decided that the arthritis in my hands, especially my right one, was going to bring my hobby to an end.

I had sold all my collections that I had made or given to others as gifts. God had brought this gift to me to share with others. It was something very personal and close to my heart. Yes, this had brought me through yet another difficult year and kept me busy with a peaceful, rewarding occupation.

During the busy month of May 2019, I had planned on visiting my son, Bryan, in Pennsylvania. I boarded the plane and took a trip by myself for the first time! How confident I had become, and how much I had grown emotionally over the last two years! I thank God for His continued grace and my faith in leading me to this point where I felt refreshed, with more wisdom each day as Jesus walked by my side.

*The Lord himself goes before you and will be with you; he will never leave you nor forsake you. Do not be afraid; do not be discouraged.* (Deuteronomy 31:8).

I shared with Bryan all these feelings I had inside. I wanted to shout them out with eager excitement. We both had so many in-depth conversations, where we spoke to one another about our most personal, intimate feelings, thoughts, and frustrations, that we both might have been keeping inside for so many years. He told me his deep memories of growing up with the needed expectations and his relationship with his dad. It was a special time together when we shared openly, throughout my time touring many areas in Pennsylvania.

On the day we finished touring an art gallery, we sat down overlooking some greenery surrounding the building. I shared with Bryan more of what I had learned and grown in reading those books that I had spoken of previously. I told him how I found it was important for a parent, once their children have grown and become independent, to release them and let them start their own life on their own. I mentioned that I did not personally take these feelings to heart before, but now I had released my parenting role.

On one of the last days we spent together, Bryan and I were talking. I told him that I often thought more about my future, which was different than I had, at times, in the past. I compared my lifestyle, back in 1984, when I had my accident, from being independent and at college, to suddenly having absolutely no freedom and confined at home. Then, when his dad, Norm, had died, I felt again that there was no reason to live because I could not do it on my own!

Through these trials and tribulations, I told Bryan how God had a reason for all that He had done and still does today, and that I just needed to keep my faith and continue to trust in Him. I also spoke of how important building boundaries are, which had taken a large place in my life ahead. I heard something from him that made my day and my vacation feel blessed. Bryan had told me he had previously bought a Bible of his own. I departed with tears, looking forward to seeing him again in September, at my home in California.

*I pray that out of his glorious riches he may strengthen you with power through his Spirit in your inner being, so that Christ may dwell in your hearts through faith. And I pray that you, being rooted and established in love, may have power, together with all the Lord's holy people to grasp how wide and long and high and deep is the love of Christ, and to know this love that surpasses knowledge—that you may be filled to the measure of all the fullness of God* (Ephesians 3:16–19).

A short time before going on this trip to see Bryan, I began writing this book you are now reading and soon will be finishing. I wrote something down that was meaningful to me while thinking back on the twenty-fifth of May, which was thirty-five years since my auto accident. Also, I realized that almost another year had passed since Norm had gone to heaven, now close to three years, as May 31 was approaching, which would have been our thirty-third anniversary. I wrote down the following thoughts…

Through wisdom (knowledge), grace, and faith I have become independent after going through trials and tribulations which I once feared fully with no future hope for me. I now have self-confidence and boundaries which are continually growing with my faith, overcoming fear and trials which God puts in my life to help me grow closer to Him each day.

Before my trip, I began attending Rose Drive Friends Church again. It had been about four years since I had been there last with Norm. I joined the Seekers Sunday school class that we belonged to for many years in the past. My eyes were still on the lookout for that special man to walk into my life, for us to build a future together.

The first Saturday of July, I remember acting as an eager and confident widow who was set to make a major decision on her own. Independently, I went to an appointment where I had a four-hour interview, which included filling out many detailed pages of membership forms, at a singles dating company. I found this on the internet while looking under "Christian Singles," or so I had thought.

Well, this was not a Christian organization, and it was here that the devil took over and began to take away my faith in God and to place another idol in charge. Sure, I still had my Christianity as the center of my life, yet at this place and time, I was sidetracked and sold on the idea that this company was the best way to plan my future.

You see, I felt so confident in myself, stepping though a little too far ahead. I entered another room after the interview process and planned to pray about my huge, important decision, which was presented to me with an astounding price, but I was swayed by the guaranteed results. I tried to pray, yet I believe my mind was already made up.

While waiting by myself in the other room, I spoke to two friends, Denise and Lisa, for their thoughts and advice. I would be spending an extremely large bulk of my savings on what I thought was a remarkable plan to meet a Christian man. Yet, even with my friends' negative feelings, I impulsively became a member of the site.

I would be set up with men to date, and I convinced myself, with the encouragement of the excessively "helpful" lady who worked with me, that a beautiful marriage was in my future. The salesperson told me there were many Christian men that I could date, and so I believed her. She tried every avenue, every fake deal she could to inspire me, and I was hooked!

You might be asking, where was that strong wisdom and discernment I had gained through books and my walk with God, over the last year or so? Yes, my self-confidence was there, but perhaps a little too much! What about the boundaries I had learned to establish and guide me?

It was as if I had forgotten how to use my faith in always trusting God *first*, before making large decisions. I headed down the wrong path and now believe that I was ripped off. I did not realize this for about six months. If only I could have read and pondered the following verse before I made that wasteful, unwise choice:

*Stay away from a fool, for you will not find knowledge on their lips* (Proverbs 14:7).

I did have a few dinner dates, with three different guys. Also, there were several other calls from various men, and although I believe now that I had strayed from God's path, I was still not afraid to share my faith. I made it clear that I was looking for someone with the same beliefs. This turned away many potential dates, and often I did not hear back from them to meet in person. I had firmly made a point to tell this company, when I signed up, that I wanted to date only Christian men.

# ⁓28⁓

# Continual Growth

In August, family came over to celebrate my dad's eightieth birthday and Laura's fifty-third. Matt and Sarah were visiting from Arizona, Brandon and Brittany were there from England, and Frank and Nichole were celebrating with us also. I wrote something special on my dad's card, that said something like this:

> Just wanted to tell you and my sis today that you both have made a strong impact in my life. I am seeing this more as I am writing my book. I wanted to let you know you mean a lot to me, and Laura made a lasting influence on me to begin my career, helping special need students.

A difficult month approached: October 2019. Even after three years, the anniversary of Norm's passing was a hard time to endure. Yes, I was attempting to date again, but Norm was such a large piece of my life that I will forever hold dear to my heart. How important was Norm in my life, and what thoughts do I have to share?

He certainly continued to encourage me and uplift my spirit, from what I had experienced from my car accident. Norm willingly helped me along the journey, one step at a time, and he accepted me, regardless of my faults or my intellect. He built up my self-esteem, my value in life, and the importance of who I was, opening me up to life's possibilities.

Norm encouraged me through difficult times when I often

was codependent or fearing confrontation. He helped me to become a strong individual who had qualities that God wanted me to share. Most importantly, he brought me closer in my relationship with my Savior, Jesus Christ. I often relate Norm's personality to the character trait of discernment: "to look at someone's character on the inside not from the outside—to show good judgment; as a Christian, to obtain spiritual guidance and understanding."

Norm and I surely tried our best to raise our children with caring minds and loving hearts. Although we learned from our mistakes, through trial and error, we also tried to serve as pleasing role models, to the best of our ability. I spoke to Brittany and Brandon, and with Matt and Sarah, at separate times in August, about their feelings of their relationship with their dad/father-in-law. Also, when Bryan was home in September before moving to Germany, I addressed the same question with Frank, Niki, and Bryan together. I asked in what ways did their father make an impact in their lives.

I first began, though, by telling them how much I had grown over the past two years with confidence and building boundaries, from books I had read, in writing my own book, and through knowledge and experience. Again, I repeated to Bryan and began sharing with Frank, Nichole, Brandon, Brittany, Matt, and Sarah how important it was to release my parenting role with them and for me to accept them moving out, on their own. I asked them also what qualities Dad had while raising them, and areas where we could have done something differently as parents. I wanted to know both the strong points and the areas I needed to work on for my future grandchildren.

In response to this, they each listed for me personality traits and qualities that made a large impact in their lives. Here are just a few of the strong character traits of their dad, or father-in-law, that they now hold close in their memory:

He taught persistence and to not give up; to be patient with their wives; to have courage and be strong; how important it was to share your faith with others and to live faithfully. They shared how their dad would tell them funny, made-up stories before bedtime; he would let them have freedom in playing outdoors with very little restrictions; and he would get up early in the morning on vacations, excited and ambitious to take them out on the lake in the boat, when the water was calm, and let the kids just have fun.

My kids also commented on a few areas that drew them further apart from us while being raised. One area was that we did not give them enough independence to let them grow up and venture ahead, as each became older. Also, many times, when Norm and I would be busy putting our efforts and time on one of the kids who was involved in sports or other activities, the others were not included, or they felt left out and alone.

I noticed on October 18, Bryan and Sarah both posted a message on Facebook of their thoughts, this third year after Norm's death. They read as follows:

Bryan:

Dad, my first week of grad school, Mom told me you were sick. Five weeks later you called while I was walking home from campus. You had stage four cancer. I ran my fingers across every single building on 34th street between Sansom and Baring to make sure it was real, that it was not a strange nightmare. You told me you loved me, that you were proud of me. Why were you talking that way? It was October 11th. I booked a trip home the next day to see you for a long weekend. But I didn't make my return flight. When I arrived, the doctors said you were not leaving that hospital room. Less than a week later, on October 18th, you left.

It happened so quickly, and nothing has felt right since. There is not a day that goes by that I do not think of you and our strange, complicated relationship. There is not a day that goes by that I do not think the world would be better off with you still in it. It is now three years later. I am back living in Germany again, the last place I shared with you while you were well and enjoying life. I wish you were here now, but I also hope to continue growing and healing a little more each year. I know it is what you would have wanted. Rest in peace, Dad.

Sarah:

Dad, these past 3 years have flown by, not a day has gone by where I have not thought about you and wished you were still here. A lot has changed in my life since then, and I can only pray/hope that you'd be proud of me. I know you'd want me to celebrate the 21 years we had together in this earthly life, so today, I'll be celebrating with one of your favorite things: a McDonald's hot fudge sundae. Love you, Dad.

Close to this time, I was very emotional during Sunday school one day. An elderly woman had a few sentimental words and shared them with me that I remember often. She was a widow and told me to have "God be my date." This made a lasting impact on me, and I still repeat it today.

Yes, it is now August 2020 as I write and am close to finishing this book. Yes, I am still single, but perhaps 2020 will be the beginning of a new book. If I look back at the end of 2019, I began listening a lot to the songs, "God Only Knows" by King and Country and "Haven't Seen It Yet" by Danny Gokey to keep myself reminded that God is always in control!

*So do not throw away your confidence; it will be richly rewarded. You need to persevere so that when you have done the will of God, you will receive what he has promised* (Hebrews 10:35–36).

You are probably wondering what ever happened to all my dates arranged through the dating site, almost six months prior. It was now the middle of December 2019, and I had dated just those three different guys, as previously mentioned. The company, whom I looked at as my idol or the key to my happy future, was not keeping the promises they had convinced me of that day when I left my faith behind and tried to follow my dreams down the wrong path.

The lady whom I spoke with or tried to contact was not returning my calls in a timely manner. I was matched with men who did not fit into my written category, as agreed upon! She told me during one of the last times we spoke that I was just "too difficult" for her to find someone who fit my "Christian" boundaries.

I met with an accountant and a lawyer who were longtime friends of mine. I was going to begin the process of bringing this company to small claims court. We had dinner and spoke of the pros and downfalls in the situation I was in. It was an exceptionally long, intense few days, trying to make the decision to proceed with a case. I needed to let go and "let God be my date." I prayed about it and wrote the following letter to the two people who were ready to stand behind me, supporting me in small claims court:

*Let the morning bring me word of your unfailing love, for I have put my trust in you. Show me the way I should go, for to you I entrust my life* (Psalm 143:8).

*I am the Lord your God, who brought you out of Egypt, out of the land of slavery. You shall have no other gods before me* (Exodus 20:2–3).

I woke up this morning and read these two verses above and after I felt my prayer was certainly answered concerning this dating site. I was feeling anxious about our conversation and what these next few months might look like and what I could be dealing with if we were to follow through in taking them to small claims court.

I made the decision six months ago to look at this singles company I found online as my "idol" and depend on them to find my "new Norm."

The most important thought is that I want to be open with others on how much this company has taken over my life, in many ways, along with a high cost involved. I want to let people be aware of this, so they do not follow the wrong path I tried to pursue.

With my accident in the past, I have a more difficult time, when being the center of attention, with my memory. As you said, I would be under oath, and I certainly don't want to say anything different than what I answered when I was taped at the interview, before signing up and paying with this dating site.

Right now, lastly, I am in the process of decreasing my seizure medication with my neurologist. I need to be careful not to be anxious or stressed out if possible.

Through all these personal reasons, I would rather just call it quits, and terminate my membership. I want to personally thank you each for your time sharing your thoughts.

Christmas 2019 is the last holiday, memories, and summaries of my life you will hear about in this book. I spent the afternoon with Frank, Nichole, Matt, and Sarah as they came to have Christmas dinner together. The grandparents could not come because my mom was extremely sick, and Sherrie was working. It was a quiet, yet relaxing Christmas. Of course, I spoke to Brandon and Brittany in England and Bryan in Germany online, so that was enjoyable. Before opening gifts and going through stockings, I read my letter to them, which I had written on December 21, when I was home by myself, about peace, joy, and hope:

PEACE  JOY  HOPE
What do these words mean to me...

*You have searched me, Lord, and you know me. You know me when I sit and when I rise; you perceive my thoughts from afar. You discern my going out and my lying down; you are familiar with all my ways. Before a word is on my tongue you, Lord, know it completely* (Psalm 139:1–4).

In the previous years, their dad, Norm, had written a letter every year at Christmastime for family and friends to read. It always seemed to have an impact on myself and many others who received the letters. This year, I felt it was my turn to take his place, in my family, to write a hopefully meaningful Christmas letter.

I began above, with a verse that truly, deeply defined where my thoughts and actions every day in every moment took place: through our Savior, Jesus Christ, our Lord, our Rock and Redeemer.

Within these past three years, I have walked and stumbled along many milestones that have brought me to where I am today. At around this same time in 2016, I felt there was not any meaningful reason for me to continue living each day alone in an unwanted path ahead of me. I didn't view any hope for my future, so very far away from this so-called joyful Christmas season, and extremely distant from the "peace" that supposedly "surpasses all understanding."

My precious family and my special friends comforted me, surrounded me with hope, and helped me with peace in situations where I felt I had no strength to continue. They each held my hands with joyful hearts, guiding me in God's footprints each day with overflowing love.

Thank you so much for being that large part of my life that I could not have filled on my own. I certainly also could not have come to where I am today without strengthening my belief in the miracle of Jesus being born in a cradle, distant, yet at peace.

Each year has become easier being alone on my journey ahead. I will forever miss my husband, Norm, your dad, your son-in-law, your brother-in-law, your brother, your uncle, your friend. Now, he too is distant, yet at peace in heaven, and I will be seeing him again someday.

After these past three years, I will end my letter on how far I have come in life's journeys and God's direction. I now feel again the joy of my everyday walk with my one and only Healer and Redeemer; my hope for the future that God has in store for me; and my peace that now deeply surpasses all my personal understanding.

Thank you all again for holding my hands tightly and staying close to my heart.

*"For I know the plans I have for you," declares the Lord, "plans to prosper you and not to harm you, plans to give you hope and a future"* (Jeremiah 29:11).

Amen and Merry Christmas,
Suzy (Mom)

P.S. "God's Not Done with You" (me) by Tauren Wells

I believe, in finishing the last fifty-five years of my life and filling many pages, I have answered the question I began this book with: "Why, God, do You put trials and tribulations in my life, and how do these moments bring me closer to You?" Last, I would like to share one more verse that summarized my Christmas letter above.

*May the God of hope fill [me] with all joy and peace as [I] trust in him, so that [I] may overflow with hope by the power of the Holy Spirit* (Romans 15:13).

# Afterword

I finished writing my book in August 2020 and began the process of trying to share these words with others. Within a week or so after, I met a Christian man on an online dating site, and this month, August 2021 we celebrated our one year anniversary of dating. He also, with a caring heart, proposed to me in June to be married in the future. I see again how God continually helps me to be patient, through *all* circumstances, and now has blessed my life once more with a special Christian man.

# About the Author

SUZANNE NORTON is a 57-year-old widow, who was blessed in raising four children and seeing God welcome into her life a precious grandson. Along with her husband, she grew strong in her faith surrounded by Christ-honoring relationships. Suzanne lives in Yorba Linda where she prays daily that she can be a humble follower of God's footprints for the future ahead.

You can contact her at Suzy.norton@gmail.com.